ORGANIZATION PLANNING
AND DEVELOPMENT

AMA RESEARCH STUDY 106

# ORGANIZATION PLANNING AND DEVELOPMENT

*William F. Glueck*

AMERICAN MANAGEMENT ASSOCIATION, INC.

© American Management Association, Inc., 1971. All rights reserved. Printed in the United States of America. Contents may not be reproduced in whole or in part without the express permission of the Association.

This Research Study has been distributed without charge to AMA members enrolled in the General Management Division.

International standard book number: 0-8144-3106-2
Library of Congress catalog card number: 78-152036

# Publisher's Foreword

This study began as a joint effort of two men: Robert D. Melcher, who was then corporate consultant on organization, North American Rockwell Corporation, and is now president of Management Responsibility Guidance Corporation; and William F. Glueck, at that time assistant professor of management, College of Business Administration, the University of Texas. Because of illness and the demands of his other professional work, Mr. Melcher was compelled to withdraw from the project, but he contributed greatly to the formulation of the study, the design of the survey, and the gathering of information through interviews.

Dr. Glueck wishes to express his gratitude to Mr. Melcher for the extensive contribution he made to this study. He also thanks Mrs. Elizabeth Hutchinson and Mrs. Barbara Watkins of the University of Missouri for their editorial and stenographic assistance, and Margaret Higginson, former AMA research program director, for her editorial guidance.

WILLIAM F. GLUECK, associate professor of management and program director, administration, for the Research Center of the School of Business and Public Administration, University of Missouri—Columbia, is on leave of absence to serve on the staff of the Industrial Administration Research Unit, The University of Aston in Birmingham, England. Dr. Glueck has served as consultant to businesses, conducted seminars, and published books and articles on organization, personnel, and business policy.

# Contents

| | |
|---|---|
| Basis of the Research | 1 |
| Highlights of the Study | 3 |
| 1. The Organization Function in Corporations | 5 |
|     Emergence of the Function | |
|     Planning and/or Development | |
|     Looking Toward the Future | |
| 2. Organization Departments and Organization Executives | 24 |
|     Companies Without Departments | |
|     Companies with Combined Departments | |
|     The Formation of Departments | |
|     The Roles of Departments | |
|     Organization Executives | |
| 3. Purposes and Objectives of the Function | 50 |
|     Goals Perceived by Presidents | |
|     Goals Perceived by Organization Executives | |
| 4. General Activities and Organization Planning | 75 |
|     Activities Reported by Company Presidents and Executives | |
|     Operating Patterns of Organization Planning | |
| 5. Organization Development and Combined Activities | 108 |
|     Operating Patterns of Organization Development | |
|     Combined Activities | |

6. Accomplishments and Challenges ..... 131
    Accomplishments of Participating Companies
    Evaluation of the Organization Function
    Problems and Challenges

Appendix A. Historical Antecedents of the Organization Function ..... 156

Appendix B. Selected Reading ..... 162

### TABLES

1. Executives responsible for the establishment of organization function in participating companies. ..... 31
2. Titles of department heads in participating companies. ..... 37
3. Reporting relationships of department heads in participating companies. ..... 38
4. Number of professionals and clerical personnel in organization departments of participating companies, industrial and nonindustrial. ..... 44
5. Organization goal statements of company presidents and organization executives. ..... 72
6. Executives whom the president consults before making decisions about 11 organization activities. ..... 76
7. Importance of 18 activities performed by organization executives and departments in participating companies. ..... 78
8. Number of participating companies performing 18 organization activities. ..... 81
9. Importance of organization activities in participating companies (ranked 1–18 by index of importance). ..... 83

### EXHIBITS

1. Position description of vice-president of organization planning (large container company). ..... 86
2. Position description of director of organization planning (large container company). ..... 87
3. Position description of manager of organization administration (large container company). ..... 87
4. Statements of organization policy, principles, and responsibilities (major airline). ..... 89

| | | |
|---|---|---|
| 5. | Position description of director of organization development (The Stanley Works). | 92 |
| 6. | Statement of services performed by organization development for divisions and corporate management (The Stanley Works). | 94 |
| 7. | Position description of corporate director of organization planning (Lockheed Aircraft Corporation). | 96 |
| 8. | Organizational relationship and responsibility, department on organization (Standard Oil Company of California). | 98 |
| 9. | Statement of functional responsibility, department on organization (Standard Oil Company of California). | 99 |
| 10. | Outlines used by department on organization to collect job information (Standard Oil Company of California). | 103 |
| 11. | Position description of director of organization planning (Kaiser Aluminum and Chemical Corporation). | 114 |
| 12. | Management responsibility guide. | 120 |
| 13. | Principles of management (medium-size metals company). | 125 |
| 14. | Principles of organization (medium-size metals company). | 127 |
| 15. | Standards of performance for managers, organization planning (Standard Oil Company [Ohio]). | 143 |

# Basis of the Research

INFORMATION for this report was obtained from a search of the literature, a research workshop, interviews, and a survey questionnaire sent to presidents and organization executives of a selected sample of companies.

The workshop was held in New York on January 20, 1967, to assist in defining the project's scope and permit an exchange of ideas among experienced executives. The session was attended by specialists on organization. Among them were James H. Davis of Aluminum Company of America, Dr. Carlos Efferson of Kaiser Aluminum and Chemical Corporation, Harvey Sherman of The Port of New York Authority, Donald Taffi of Electro-Optical Systems Division, Xerox Corporation, and William F. Wrightnour of UniRoyal, Incorporated. The workshop was recorded, and portions of the discussions are presented in this report.

Several questionnaires were tested, and on May 26, 1967, a president's questionnaire and a staff executive's questionnaire were sent to 1,242 presidents of companies listed in *Fortune*'s 1966–1967 *Plant and Product Directory* of the 1,000 largest U.S. industrial corporations and 250 largest nonmanufacturers (the top 50 commercial banks, life insurance companies, merchandising firms, transportation companies, and utilities). Responses were received from 209 companies.

In classifying responses to the questionnaire, various methods were tried. Because many companies have multiple products and services, classification by industry was impractical. The *Fortune* companies are ranked by volume of sales; other possible rankings are by assets and by number of employees. Since a fairly close similarity

1

exists in these three methods, *Fortune*'s classifications based on sales volume were used. Two groups are the typical breakdown for *Fortune*'s top 500 industrials: large firms (ranked 1–250) and medium-size firms (251–500). For the AMA study a third category—smaller industrials, ranked 501–1,000 in the *Fortune* listing—was added. The 250 nonmanufacturers were the basis for AMA's list of nonindustrials; all are large companies.

Of the 209 companies responding, 67 are large; 42 are medium-size; and 55 are smaller. All these firms are industrial. Forty-five are nonindustrial companies.

One hundred sixty-nine presidents and 115 organization planning and development executives returned usable questionnaires. In 91 companies both the president and the organization executive completed questionnaires. Thirty-eight companies preferred to respond by letter. Responses were received from companies in the three size groups in the numbers shown in the accompanying tabulation.

|  | Questionnaires |  |  |  |
| --- | --- | --- | --- | --- |
| Company size | Presidents | Organization Executives | Both | Letters |
| Industrials |  |  |  |  |
| Large | 42 | 39 | 25 | 18 |
| Medium-size | 35 | 33 | 20 | 7 |
| Smaller | 51 | 15 | 18 | 8 |
| Nonindustrials | 41 | 28 | 28 | 5 |
| Totals | 169 | 115 | 91 | 38 |

In addition to the ten companies represented at the research workshop, 12 other companies with effective organization departments cooperated through interviews. These interviews, most often conducted with organization executives but in several cases including the president, were two to five hours in length.

An examination of the responses indicated that most industries and company sizes were represented in the returns. The interviews were chosen to present cases of outstanding practice which are not to be considered representative of practices in the field today.

All quotations attributed to a person or company are used with the permission of the participating executive or company.

# Highlights of the Study

This study found that many large firms have formed organization planning and development departments since the late 1950s. A large number of medium-size firms also provide for organization planning and development, but usually they combine this function with personnel or corporate planning. Frequently, the function developed in conjunction with a change in top management or prior to a major change in organization structure.

Many managers of organization planning and development departments report to top management. They head a relatively small department—seven professionals or fewer—and they usually have college and graduate degrees with job experience in staff functions, especially in personnel administration. The goals of the department, and the reasons for its coming into existence, usually emphasize contribution to corporate objectives by building an effective organization structure and developing an effective management team that will create a healthy organization climate. To achieve these objectives, the departments perform activities appropriate to their orientation.

Organization-planning departments (1) establish guidelines for analyzing, evaluating, and developing sound and effective organization structures; (2) perform organization studies and recommend changes in existing organization structures; (3) help clarify roles and responsibilities of individuals and departments.

Organization-development departments (1) conduct organization studies and recommend changes in existing organization structure and climate; (2) recommend methods and programs to improve interpersonal and intergroup relations, effectiveness, and company work climate; (3) develop methods and programs to strengthen leadership and managerial skills, and provide for managerial succession and compensation plans.

The study found that the departments' accomplishments parallel the objectives set for them. Typical results listed by corporate presidents or departments include (1) corporate reorganization plans that make the company more effective or efficient; (2) improved management skills to fit the company's current organization philosophy; (3) the creation of a new organizational climate for the firm.

Of the two approaches to the organization function, organization planning is favored by The Standard Oil Company of California, Lockheed Aircraft Corporation, and The Stanley Works. These companies have chosen the older, traditional approach that is preferred by a majority of organization departments. In this method, structure and other formal organization factors are emphasized, and abilities, attitudes, and relationships of the individuals in the departments are generally given less emphasis.

Companies using the second, newer method of organization development include UniRoyal and Kaiser. The development approach followed by these firms integrates formal organization factors with people-oriented activities such as team development and group-goals determination, within a specified work climate, for the purpose of achieving the organization's objectives.

Most departments naturally combine the two approaches to some extent. Organization authorities observe a significant shift toward more people-oriented, behavioral activities in organization-planning departments. And, although there are comparatively few full-fledged organization-development departments in the United States today, the author believes that the number will grow. This will come about in one of three ways: (1) expansion and enlargement of the scope of organization-planning departments; (2) mergers of some aspects of personnel with organization-planning activities, resulting in a new type of organization function; or (3) establishment by top management of new organization-development departments.

# 1. The Organization Function in Corporations

Today in industry, government, and nonprofit fields, people talk about organization, communication, and human relations as never before. Most studies of firms and their top management problems show that organization and human problems are uppermost in the minds of top executives. A study reported in *Dun's Review* found corporate presidents particularly concerned with three types of problems: marketing strategy, organization planning, and research and development management.[1] Countless sources support this concern with organization today.

Not only are most modern firms growing in size and complexity much more rapidly than in the past; executives and employees are much better educated and, with their increased knowledge of the behavioral sciences, are more skilled in problem solving.

### Emergence of the Function

In the past 50 years major changes have taken place in industrial organization, paralleling the growth in the size and complexity of American firms. In the early 1900s line managers regarded organization as an integral part of the manager's job. After all, the literature of the time told them that managers were expected to plan, organize, staff, direct, and control their departments or firms. As companies grew larger and more complex, they began to encounter organization problems. Often they established ad hoc committees to solve a specific problem and dissolved the committee when the task had been completed. Sometimes, line executives or committees responsible for organization would seek the advice of outside consultants during the decision-making process.

As often happened with staff services, increased need for advice and assistance resulted in the formation of internal staff groups in some companies. These groups then developed into organization departments. Frequently, they evolved from personnel departments, but occasionally they sprang up in other departments or were started as separate units.

Before World War II few companies had organization departments. One of the first—if not the very first—was established in 1931 at Standard Oil Company of California. Since then, the activity has gained greater acceptance among corporations. Most of the organization planning and development departments of the companies that participated in this study were formed in the late 1950s and 1960s.

The smaller the firm, the more recent is the establishing of the function. More than half of the companies participating in the study set it up after 1960; moreover, all the smaller firms established it since that time.

Marvin R. Weisbord, a consultant, states that firms are looking at organization and are willing to experiment with organization development for the following reasons:

Inflation and the threat of recession, which raise costs and squeeze profits, push management toward the use of any new knowledge that might increase effectiveness.

Recognition is growing that improved technology requires better human capabilities.

There is relatively less room for improvement in the highly rationalized and sophisticated systems used for managing physical assets—equipment, land, buildings, and cash—than in the still primitive area of organizing people for work, giving them tools, and rewarding them for their contributions.

In the past decade greatly improved ways of studying and measuring the human organization and its internal changes have developed.

In addition to better measuring rods, there is an evolving and increasingly effective technology of organization development.[2]

The function has been growing, partly because corporation presidents believe that organization is a very important determinant of corporate success. The extent of their involvement in the activity is confirmed by the survey conducted for this report. Of 167 presidents who participated, 51 percent (84) reported that they spend more than 11 percent of their time on organization problems. Thirty-three percent (56) spend 5 to 10 percent of their time on such problems. Only 16 percent (27) of the presidents devote less than 5 percent of their time to organization problems. The percentage of time thus occupied by presidents in companies of varying size was reported as follows:

| Time spent by presidents on organization problems | Large Percent | Large No. | Medium-size Percent | Medium-size No. | Small Percent | Small No. | Totals Per-cent | Totals No. of companies |
|---|---|---|---|---|---|---|---|---|
| Less than 5 percent | 20 | 15 | 12 | 4 | 14 | 8 | 16 | 27 |
| 5 to 10 percent | 39 | 29 | 41 | 14 | 22 | 13 | 33 | 56 |
| 11 to 20 percent | 31 | 23 | 35 | 12 | 47 | 28 | 38 | 63 |
| More than 20 percent | 10 | 7 | 12 | 4 | 17 | 10 | 13 | 21 |
|  | 100 | 74 | 100 | 34 | 100 | 59 | 100 | 167 |

In the surveyed companies that have an organization department, the presidents spend some of their time with the department directors and are able to devote less time to solving organization problems.

In two-thirds of the companies, the president or chairman of the board initiated the departments. An even larger proportion of smaller firms' and nonindustrial firms' departments was founded by these top executives.

Eighty-eight percent (137) of 156 departments of participating companies were formed by vice-presidents or higher executives, a figure that suggests that the departments received some top management support, at least at one time. Many departments were formed when there was a change in the corporate presidency or in the firm's environment.

In a study of the 100 largest corporations (1962–1964), D. Ronald Daniel of McKinsey and Company found that 66 of the firms mentioned in their annual reports that they had realigned their organization structures.[3] Furthermore, as a result of 200 major organization studies, Daniel observed that the large firms had experienced a major organization change every two years; Daniel concluded that the larger the firm, the more likely it is to change.[4]

The need to analyze an organization becomes more apparent as the firm becomes larger and more complex. Failure to analyze causes companies to become rigid and unable to adapt to their environment. John W. Gardner, in discussing company organization in his book, *Self Renewal: The Individual and the Innovative Society*, implies the need for organization departments:

> The same flexibility and adaptiveness that we seek for the society as a whole are essential for the organizations within the society. A society made of arteriosclerotic organizations cannot renew itself. ...
>
> Perhaps the most distinctive thing about innovation today is that we are beginning to pursue it systematically. The large corporation does not set up a research laboratory to solve a specific problem, but to engage in continuous innovation. That is good renewal doctrine. But such laboratories usually limit their innovative efforts to products and processes. What may be most in need of innovation is the corporation itself. Perhaps what every corporation needs is a department of continuous renewal that would view the whole organization as a system in need of continuing innovation.[5]

## Planning and/or Development

Organization planning and development is a function whose purpose is to help the company achieve its goals by providing it with an effective organization structure and work climate. This can be achieved in the company by a department or group staffed by professionals and supplemented from time to time by consultants.

### Basic Approaches

Two different perspectives on this function are identified in the organization-planning approach and the organization-development approach. The first can best be explained by a brief example.

When organization executives are called in to study a problem whose symptoms have been diagnosed as possibly caused by organization, several sets of tools can be used to analyze the problem. One set involves a scientific study of the formal relationship between people and departments as prescribed by the company. This set of relationships is called the organization structure.

Structural analysis requires study of the formal mechanisms used to divide up the work and to provide coordination among the parts. An analyst examines the activities of individuals, units, and departments; the grouping of these activities; the levels in the hierarchy; the roles of the groups in relation to each other; and the organization's centralization—all within the context of the company's size and the complexity of its business.

With regard to coordination and control, the analyst needs to examine executive responsibility, delegation of authority, span of control, and the use of special coordinators or coordinating groups such as committees or task forces. He may also examine whether staffs are used effectively for coordination and control and determine whether conflict between line and staff is excessive.

Thus the organization planner is concerned with developing and maintaining an organization structure that is effective for the company, considering its size, complexity, and corporate strategy. He is aware of the human beings staffing the structure but tends to expect them to adapt to the structure designed for the department or firm. In this study his approaches and tools, together with their paperwork implementation (organization charts, organization manuals, job descriptions, and so forth), are called structural activities.

A different approach is taken by the organization-development specialist. His emphasis is on people and their relationships. He believes that formal structure is less important than the human beings in it and that the structure should be adapted to human relationships. Executives who use this approach tend to feel that an organization cannot be really analyzed without considering the attitudes and orientations of the people in it, and also the working climate within the firm.

Many organization analysts believe that organizations develop personalities of their own, independent of the persons who work in those firms. Sometimes this occurs because of the leadership and values of strong executives in the past—historical factors that are reflected in personnel policies and practices, norms of appropriate behavior for executives, and the like. Norms and attitudes about work and the organization can be perpetuated by several subsequent generations of executives.

Organization analysts point out that to apply universal principles of organization to a company, without considering that company's work climate, is a disservice to the organization process. These analysts show great concern for the satisfaction of the people with the structure; they emphasize informal, nonprogrammed coordination mechanisms by building them on the attitudes and informal practices of the department or firm. Frequently, they use modified T-groups, group goal setting, and other quasi-training devices to help implement new organizational relationships; they formalize the relationships by building on the informal structure. These activities and other related ones described in this study are called behavioral or "people" activities.

During the AMA research workshop conducted for this study, Robert D. Melcher, president of Management Responsibility Guidance Corporation, defined the two approaches as follows:

There are two different approaches: organization planning, which focuses on the analysis aspect, and organization development, the guidance aspect, which often involves resolving sensitive interpersonal and intergroup relationship problems.

Organization planning is involved with reviewing and evaluating, on a continuing basis, all organization entities to determine whether the missions, structures, functions, and responsibility relationships are clearly defined and understood and effectively coordinated to facilitate the overall objectives of the company.

Organization development is providing counsel and guidance that aid and encourage management to develop and clarify its organizational missions; to delineate and effectively group the work to be performed; and to clarify and resolve responsibility relationships that will enable both the organization and its people to realize their mutual objectives.

In summary, *organization planning* is an approach to organization problems that places primary emphasis on structural activities and formal analysis of the structure as a means to improve or maintain an effective organization for the company. *Organization development* is an approach to organization problems that places primary emphasis on behavioral or people activities in attempting to integrate the informal and formal organizations for corporate effectiveness. These terms are often used interchangeably, but the author considers the two approaches to be different and distinguishes between them throughout this report.

## Views of Authorities on Organization

Specialists in organization planning and development expressed their views of the two approaches at the AMA workshop.

Harvey Sherman, director of the department of organization and procedures at The Port of New York Authority, spoke for the organization-planning approach:

Too many people think that organization means only boxes on an organization chart. Organizing is much more than formal structure. It has to take into account all interrelationships, formal or informal, and all kinds of human relations, such as how people work together in an organization. This is much more than mere structure. However, organization does not include the usual functions of personnel administration—industrial relations, recruitment, selection, pay plans, retirement plans, and so forth. These things are not included in my concept of organization planning.

Basically, organization is dividing up work to achieve the short- and long-term goals of the enterprise. It includes the development of people and must be related to profits and other goals. But, basically, it is dividing up the work.

Paul Lawrence, a professor at Harvard University Graduate School of Business Administration, stated his position regarding the organization-development approach:

The term "organization development" should have more emphasis on "development." The future-oriented design of all the human aspects of organization—any future organizational system—has to hook into the economic system, the technical system, and other things to which people contribute. But it can be separated from the present system in terms of known manpower needs and recruitment, and replacement and training needs.

E. I. du Pont de Nemours & Company uses the organization-development approach described by Robert L. Hershey:

All human organizations have three essential features. First, they have an objective—a result to be achieved. Second, there are people, the implements by which the organization gets its work done and produces the results which are the reason for its existence. Third, there is the way the people are placed in working relationship with each other. For greatest effectiveness, both the people and the structure of the organization must be well tuned to its objectives. The people will need to have whatever special skills are required, and the structure must bring the people together in a way which stimulates maximum use of those skills on the essentials of the job to be done. Proper structure provides for doing those things necessary to attain the objective and at the same time firmly excludes the doing of those things which are unnecessary.

... Thus, if the organizational planning is an activity having as its purpose the preparation for those changes which will be necessary to keep the organization at top efficiency, it will be seen that it must certainly concern itself with the problem of people, perhaps much of the time with organizational structure, and probably even now and then with a reexamination of broad objectives.

Mr. Hershey pointed out that, contrary to what many people think, the establishment of an organization-planning department does not necessarily result in a more formal company. One can formally organize for informality or for any purpose—for exercise of initiative or restriction of it, for centralization or decentralization, for slow or fast action, for controlled or uncontrolled management. One can even organize systematically for chaos instead of order. In fact, some organizations do this to create stress situations that would test key men under circumstances of emergency and confusion. The point is that organization planning involves a formalization, or increase in systematic attention, in deciding how to organize to get a thing done. It does not require that what is done as a result of the planning be formally structured.[6]

## *Accomplishments and Challenges*

Different types of accomplishments can result from organization planning and organization development. Typical organization-planning accomplishments include improved organization structure, as in the case of decentralized divisions; reduction in personnel, resulting from organization-structure surveys; and more clear-cut delegation of authority. Organization-development accomplishments include integration of company organization change with new organization policy; development programs on group goal setting and leadership; assistance in creating new managerial environment and organization needed for future growth.

Evaluation of the organization planning and development function is considered important by many companies. Organization executives participating in this study stated that they submit reports to help evaluate the function in 55 percent (23) of 42 large participating industrial and nonindustrial companies, 67 percent (14) of 21 medium-size industrial companies, and 72 percent (26) of 36 smaller companies.

Presidents said that they themselves evaluate the organization function in 57 percent (43) of 75 large industrial and nonindustrial companies, 64 percent (21) of 33 medium-size industrials, and 50 percent (22) of 44 smaller industrials. Only 36 presidents indicated that they use general, oral reviews; 41, that they make formal, written evaluations. The basis of the evaluation tends to be overall effectiveness as perceived by the top executives to whom the function reports.

Corporate presidents focus on effective goal achievement—that is, results—regarding organization. They want effective managers who can deal with real organization problems—lack of organization policies, or difficulty in providing organization structure in a rapidly changing world, for example. But department heads focus on means, such as influencing other managers with their work.

This study makes one fact very clear: An effective organization planning and development department must be perceived as an aid in problem solving. Effective departments begin by helping with small organization problems and work their way up to greater problems. Since relationships are critical to the activity, effective department heads try to establish rapport with line executives. This is the key to effectiveness for such a staff activity as organization planning and development.

*Goals and Orientation*

Both the presidents and the organization department heads submitted statements of goals for their companies' organization planning and development. Goals indicate the focus of the function and serve as evaluative mechanisms of the department's activities and accomplishments.

The company presidents presented goal statements of two basic types: specific departmental goals of organization planning and organization development; and general goal statements, which equated organization department goals with personnel department goals or company goals.

The specific goals most frequently cited were as follows: (1) to build an effective organization structure (organization planning); (2) to build effective management teams; (3) to integrate the first two goals (organization development). These goal statements reflect the types of activities conducted by the departments. Twenty-six percent (43) of 167 presidents responding gave goal statements that reflect an organization-development approach. Seventeen percent (28) of these presidents listed organization-planning goals.

Other goal statements made by the presidents were the same as those of other departments or the firm, or at least similar to them. One-fourth of the presidents indicated that they believe the goals of the organization department are the same as those of an effective personnel department. This frequently is the opinion where the firm has a combined organization and personnel department. Ten percent of the presidents supplied goal statements that could apply to a corporate-planning department; a number of these firms have a combined organization–corporate-planning department. Twelve percent of the presidents gave the same goals for the department as for the firm.

The goals listed by the heads of the organization departments ranged from a few statements of job functions to well-delineated objectives similar to those listed by the presidents. Forty-three percent (48) of 112 department heads listed organization-planning goals. Twenty percent (22) of these executives gave organization-development goals similar to those of personnel departments; these frequently are used by combined organization and personnel departments. Thirteen percent listed goal statements similar to those of corporate planning departments; again, many were from organization–corporate planning departments. Only 91 of the responding companies provided responses from both the president and the organization department head.

Most of the presidents who stated their company goals do not have an organization department. A much greater percentage of department heads than presidents stated organization-planning goals. This situation is mentioned in earlier literature and indicates that many organization-planning departments are not well supported by the presidents as organization development departments.

## Departmental Activities

Corporate organization executives were asked to indicate which activities they or their organization departments performed, and which were the most important. These judgments were combined, and the activities were classified in three categories: (1) highly important, (2) moderately important, and (3) least important to all the participating companies.

The three activities rated as *highly important* by all companies were as follows: (1) recommending methods and programs to improve interpersonal and intergroup relations and the company's work climate; (2) developing plans for managerial succession and relating them to corporate plans for expansion or contraction; (3) developing managerial compensation and incentive programs.

Three activities rated as *moderately important* by companies of all sizes were the following: (1) establishing guidelines for analyzing, evaluating, and developing sound and effective organization; (2) evaluating and making recommendations for proposed organization changes; (3) conducting organization studies and recommending changes to improve the existing organization.

Rated as *least important* by companies of all sizes were these three: (1) preparing, distributing, and maintaining a manual of organization charts, position descriptions, and related guides; (2) providing assistance in the preparation of organization charts and position descriptions; (3) providing advice concerning the implementation of organization changes approved by management.

A comparison of the ratings by company size disclosed that four activities were considered more important in the larger companies, declined in importance in medium-size firms, and were even less important in smaller firms: (1) auditing structures, procedures, supervisory ratios, and management levels for compliance to company policy; (2) recommending methods and programs to strengthen leadership and improve managerial skills in problem solving, group goal setting, and the like; (3) recommending organization department objectives and policies to top management; (4) developing plans for identifying, appraising, and increasing the growth of high-potential management talent.

Three activities were rated as relatively unimportant by the larger companies but were considered more important in the smaller firms: (1) assisting management in the functions of identification, definition, and grouping necessary to meet management's objectives; (2) helping management clarify the roles and the responsibility relationships of individuals and groups; (3) advising management concerning organization department objectives, plans, and policies.

In general, the larger participating companies give priority to developing corporation objectives, improving organization effectiveness, modifying or otherwise changing the corporate organization structure, and determining compensation of key executives. Larger and smaller companies emphasize the establishment of organization policies but seem unconcerned about managerial-succession plans and the definition and assignment of key roles. Medium-size companies take the reverse position. All participating companies agreed that evaluation of mergers and acquisitions is the least relevant activity for organization departments.

*Combined-Function Departments*

Among 59 participating companies that combined organization with other functions, 81 percent (48) of the joint departments included personnel; 10 percent (6), corporate planning; and 7 percent (4), administration. Most of these companies were medium-size, and a few were small. Examples of each type of joint department are presented in later chapters of this report.

Combined-function departments provide services similar to those of separate organization departments. They tend to operate in either organization planning or organization development, as do the separate departments. Depending on the size of the subunit and the orientation of its overall department, the functions can become submerged beneath the other staff services; or they can grow for the benefit of the corporation.

Organization units of combined departments can experience severe difficulties. Their status and usefulness tend to reflect the status of the department. If the organization department is part of a personnel department that is basically oriented toward blue collar workers or record keeping, the organization unit may experience difficulty in performing creative activities. Top managers are likely to believe that a unit so composed is unable to deal with corporate organization problems. The result is that the scope of organization is reduced to minor organization studies. In this case, the organization section probably should attempt to separate itself from the department.

The reverse is also true. If personnel is a dynamic, well-regarded function that has made historical contributions to a firm's activities and is led by capable and influential executives, the organization unit's contributions can be enhanced and its usefulness expanded.

## Looking Toward the Future

Organization planning and development as a company activity seems to show greater promise for the future than it has up to now. Although a few companies have dropped the function, a larger number seem to be adopting or expanding it. TRW, Texas Instruments Corporation, Federated Department Stores, American Airlines, and several other major corporations are thoroughly involved in organization activities. The U.S. Air Force has been formalizing the function and has hired the holder of a Ph.D. degree from Massachusetts Institute of Technology's Sloan School of Management to head the unit. More and more techniques are being taught by universities, the National Training Laboratory, and management education institutions. Practitioners are being trained in modern organization theory —a vast improvement over past teaching.

The future of organization planning and development depends upon executive acceptance and awareness of the need for analysis and improvement of organization structure and environment. These factors are influenced by prevailing organization theories, which are expressed as two almost opposite concepts.

*Classical concept.* The first of the two approaches to organization theory follows principles of organization and assumes that organizations in all fields of endeavor will be effective if they adopt what the sociologists call the bureaucratic model of organization. Some management authorities, such as Douglas McGregor, note that advocates of this position have rather pessimistic views about human nature. Followers of this approach advocate a very structured organization: clear and definite position descriptions, careful definition of authority and responsibility relationships, line and staff distinctions, small spans of control, and so forth. They see future organizations developed and staffed as they are today, or even more rigid and more effectively centralized and controlled. Some advocates of the classical approach contend that organizations of the future will be still larger because of growth, mergers, conglomerates, the requirements of technology, and other factors.

Acceptance of this position suggests a greater need for organization planning and development, but with an accompanying need to understand the potentials of computer methods and various techniques that permit increased control. Because of size, complexity, and change factors, organization executives of this future world probably would be planners rather than developmental specialists.

*Behavioral concept.* The second approach to organization theory is based on the assumption that bureaucratic and structured organizations are inappropriate in our present society because they do not permit changes in persons and human relations. This position is best exemplified in the work of Warren G. Bennis, professor and provost at the State University of New York at Buffalo. In his book *Changing Organizations* Dr. Bennis argues that structured organizations do not allow for the development of people and are slow to adapt to change. He predicts that future organizations will be staffed by better-educated people, desirous of personal growth, who have rejected or become indifferent to the work values of the Protestant ethic. Rapid technological change will lead to closer links between government and business, interdependence of organizations and sciences, and shorter product and service lines. This environment demands fluid, temporary organizations, Dr. Bennis argues. Bureaucracy might have been effective in a stable world with large numbers of uneducated workers, but in his opinion it will not be so in the new world ahead and will die out.[7]

To cope with this type of environment, companies require help from organization development specialists.

## Organization—A Growth Function

Despite differences in concepts, one factor seems clear: Organization planning and development is a growth function. At the research workshop held in New York City for this study, Paul Lawrence, professor at Harvard Business School, said that

> organization planning and development is going to be a most important function in the next decade or two. I think it will become a key competitive difference between companies and institutions.
>
> In my opinion, one of the great issues is: Can we design institutions that will tackle new problems we have to face as a society? It is terribly important that we learn how to improve our ability to design organizations that will do what they set out to do, or to design and invent new organizational forms for doing new kinds of tasks.

In the future, most organizations will be involved in products and services that are volatile, and although many aspects of the corporation's work will be in flux, others will still be relatively routine. The challenge to organization analysts is to assess the present and future states of the system and subsystems and recommend appropriate structural and behavioral adjustments to make these systems more effective and efficient. This approach is usually called the "contingency" or "conditional" approach. As Dr. Lawrence pointed out:

> The one thing that most behavioral scientists seem to agree on today is that we should stop the search for universal answers to organization problems. Today we're much more oriented toward contingency and conditional studies. I think this is a very encouraging trend. It will generate some knowledge, and some transducers through communication channels; so the knowledge will be useful. And I think some things are coming along that organization people will find more useful than things they have had in the past, particularly in the macroscopic area.
>
> The day is coming when there will be an avenue for doing more systematic teaching to prepare people for organization work. Today people come from different backgrounds; they learn from their own experience how to get things done by

going ahead and doing them. This apprenticeship system won't change overnight, but sooner or later it should give way to more systematic training.

A good start has already been made with Fred E. Fiedler's research in leadership, the work of Paul Lawrence and Jay Lorsch at Harvard Business School, Joan Woodward's research at Imperial College, the work of the Tavistock Institute, and that of Derek Pugh and his associates at London Graduate School of Business Studies. These studies give hope for the future. More generally known is the persuasive work of the behavioral-science group, oriented toward the fluid organization, that gives us insights into this method of organization—the Likert group at the University of Michigan; Daniel Katz, Robert Kahn, and Dorwin Cartwright; the M.I.T. group (Warren Bennis, Edgar Schein, Mason Haire, and Chris Argyris); the UCLA (University of California at Los Angeles) group (Robert Tannenbaum and his associates); Abraham Zaleznick; Herbert Shepard; Harold Leavitt; and Robert Blake.

The classical theorists—Ernest Dale, Joseph Litterer, and the teams of Peter Blau and William Scott, and Eliot Chapple and Leonard Sayles—also illuminate this approach. Some of the younger organization men have learned their specialty through books—for example, *Handbook on Organizations*, edited by James March—and from journals such as *Administrative Science Quarterly*. The field has already expanded far.

The author believes that an evolutionary process is occurring and that, in the future, dynamic firms will make more use of organization-development analysts and techniques, and more stable firms will be using organization planners and structural-change methods. Well-trained organization planners will realize there are two distinct types of organization environment: the volatile, changing companies or divisions and the stabilized, mature companies or divisions. Planners will be able to hire the proper type of individual to fit the company's environment and will work to create an environment suitable for the individuals in the company. Furthermore, if changes in the environment are needed, really effective firms and planners will encourage them. They will be concerned not only about the company's needs and resources but also about the individual's needs and abilities. It is likely that the individual's abilities will vary during his lifetime and enable him to have several careers. This development should lead to increased productivity in companies.

## Directors Predict Future Trends

Several directors of organization departments have predicted the future of the function. Carlos Efferson, vice-president of organization planning at Kaiser, sees the future as bright because specialists in the field are now better-trained:

I think we've learned a lot and are getting to where we know how to approach an organization study. We are much more sophisticated about the interrelationships of formal structure with the behavioral sciences. There are now hundreds of persons who not only know organization analysis but know all the arguments, pro and con, of the various types of organization analysis. Twelve years ago, when I surveyed the field, I could almost number the organization specialists on the fingers of my hand.

Harvey Sherman, manager of organization planning at The Port of New York Authority, agrees with Dr. Efferson:

Organization development is getting more long-range oriented. I think there's more recognition that what we do today will affect what is going to happen ten years from now. Organization people are now taking into account the new systems approach, automation, the behavioral-science discoveries, and so on. It's a more complex job than it used to be. Furthermore, organization development is becoming more pervasive. It's growing. I expect that in the future there will be more and more people in the field.

The organization director at Bank of America believes that organization can be a dynamic function if it is modernized. He says:

The role of organization planning is changing—there are more forecasting and forward thinking, more long-range planning, and more evaluation of planning.

Organization planning is getting more and more into other aspects of business, such as marketing. For example, the organizational impact of automation on banking needs to be more fully explored. The business environment is changing, and we feel we should take the initiative by aiding executives in management to determine whether Bank of America's concept of branch banking should be modified.

How can organization planning help management to understand and react to customers in order to better serve the needs? Since business is becoming more sophisticated, organization planners must find ways of making total resources of banks available to customers and showing them how best to use the funds.

Frank Piersol, manager of the department on organization at Standard Oil Company of California, sees few changes for the future development of his department:

I see no major changes in approach to organization planning. Prior to 1963, our department was conducting organization surveys primarily on a request basis; today we are conducting surveys of all major company units on a continuing and programmed basis. It is a way of life—and there is a definite trend of increased requests for our services from subsidiary companies.

Executives are becoming more and more business-oriented and, because of the squeeze on profits, are increasingly concerned with costs. In our company, future executives are serving on the survey teams. We find that it is a tremendous executive development process. But, basically, we see no significant changes coming in the manner in which we conduct our organization activities. There will be a continued development of new and improved organization patterns, as needed, to meet changes in the nature of our business and its workload. Organization planning must be dynamic.

Donald Taffi, formerly director of organization at Electro-Optical Systems, predicts more emphasis on the organization-development approach. Mr. Taffi explained his viewpoint as follows:

One aspect that will be more important in the future is behavioral characteristics. These "people aspects" will be emphasized a great deal more. I think that this is a trend and that it is emerging because the means for accomplishing things in terms of facilities, dollars, and so forth are such equalizers today that the only real difference is resources. In other words, a major factor is the company's ability to come up with new product ideas to meet the demands, wherever they happen to be. This ability is completely dependent on the people. So I think people are the real factor that make organization planning complex and will make it more complex in the future.

In summary, organization planning and development will be one of the most promising and rewarding fields available to companies in the future. Top management awareness of what these staff activities can do for a firm should encourage the establishment and growth of organization departments in many, if not most, successful American corporations.

### REFERENCES

1. "America's Best-Managed Companies," *Dun's Review and Modern Industry* (September 1960), p. 40.
2. Marvin R. Weisbord, "What, Not Again! Manage People Better?" *Think* (January–February 1970), pp. 2–9.
3. D. Ronald Daniel, "Reorganizing for Results," *Harvard Business Review* (November–December 1966), pp. 96–104.
4. Ibid.
5. John W. Gardner, *Self Renewal: The Individual and the Innovative Society* (New York: Harper & Row, 1963).
6. Robert L. Hershey, "Organization Planning," *MSU Business Topics* (Winter 1962), pp. 29–40.
7. Warren G. Bennis, *Changing Organizations* (New York: McGraw–Hill, 1966).

# 2. Organization Departments and Organization Executives

ORGANIZATIONAL problems of business and industry are solved in numerous ways and vary considerably from company to company. Several general patterns were found in this study. The formation of a separate organization planning and development department is a method commonly used by large companies. Medium-size firms tend to set up joint departments, combining organization activities with some related function such as personnel. When neither of these methods suits a particular company, it may delegate the work to line managers or hire a consulting firm to solve its immediate problems.

Of 205 companies participating in this study, 81 have a separate organization department; 59 have a combined department (organization and other activities); 16 are planning to set up such a department; and 49 have no department and no plans to set one up at this time. Eighty percent of the largest firms (ranked by sales) reported having an organization department, but only about 14 percent of the smallest firms have such a department. Only 18 percent of the largest firms lack a department, but well over 70 percent of the companies with lower sales volumes have no separate department. Evidently, smaller firms find separate departments uneconomical and use other methods to perform organization activities.

An examination of the data shows that companies with very high or very low sales volumes do not have combined or joint departments. Most joint departments were found in companies with sales volumes of $100 million to $275 million. Professor Joseph Bailey, in the early 1960s, also found that large companies had separate departments and medium-size companies often had combined departments.[1] This pattern probably exists for other new staff functions as well.

Of the 45 participating nonindustrial firms—all of which are large—25 now have or are planning to create a separate department; 15 have a joint department; and only 5 reported no department. Most of the insurance companies, banks, and retailing companies have an organization department. Transportation and utility companies have a somewhat smaller percentage of organization departments than the other nonindustrials.

## Companies Without Departments

If a company does not cope with organization planning and development problems by setting up either a separate or a joint department for this purpose, it substitutes other methods. Prior to this study, the author hypothesized that companies used three such substitutes: outside consultants, line managers, and ad hoc committees or temporary task forces composed of operating executives and established to handle specific problems. The responses of companies that have no organization departments confirmed the accuracy of these hypotheses, and the data helped clarify the reasons for the choice of method.

Only one company said it used outside consultants as a primary means of solving organization problems. A few chiefly used ad hoc committees. D. L. Roskam, president of Cessna Aircraft Corporation, stated his company's approach succinctly: "Organization planning and development in our company is part of the responsibility of our corporate-planning committee function, which includes divisional operating heads and group vice-presidents."

An executive of a medium-size steel company explained his firm's position:

We do not have a staff executive or department for organization planning and development. Practically all the growth we have experienced has been internal. We handle organization matters through the medium of management conferences in which the executive personnel concerned participate. We have not employed outside counsel for this purpose because we have had no need for this kind of help, up to now.

One group of responding companies reported that their top managers consider organization planning to be a top management function. Henry R. Roberts, president, Connecticut General Life Insurance Company, said:

> We do not have one executive assigned this responsibility. Our vice-president and actuary and our personnel vice-president handle the most important segments of this work, and I spend 5 to 10 percent of my time working with them.

And R. Stanley Laing, president of National Cash Register Company, reported that in his company

> fundamental organization planning and development is done by executive management, including our key operating officers. Resolving organizational questions concerning any one division is considered a primary responsibility of that division's management.

Finally, the president of a medium-size steel company said of his firm's practice in this regard: "The president and chairman of the board have a keen interest in this function, and they make certain it gets adequate attention without a formal organization department."

Another group of companies indicated that organization planning and development is one of the functions of its line managers, not a staff function. For example, John Hickey, formerly vice-president of planning at Motorola, Inc., explained: "We do not have a separate department because we believe that this is an important and inseparable part of the responsibility of every operating executive and manager."

A spokesman for a small manufacturing company said: "We firmly believe that responsibility for this function belongs with line organization, with assistance from staff groups." And W. C. Norris, president of Control Data Corporation, explained: "Organization is defined by operating executives within broad policies and approved by higher levels of management."

Some companies reporting were quite emphatic on this point. Stephen Gardner, president of Girard Trust Bank, said that his firm has no department because "it is our intention to motivate, rather than administer." A spokesman for a packaging firm said that his company is not large enough to have a department; but, he added, "The function is too important to trust to specialists."

Finally, several companies explained that because they use decentralized and/or divisionalized organization structures, the corporate headquarters maintain no organization departments.

L. B. Hunter, vice-president of administration, Inland Steel Corporation, explained that the decentralized divisions in his company perform organization jobs.

Each of our major departments and divisions and subsidiaries is responsible for its own organizational planning and development; and this is coordinated and approved by our three general executives, who in turn play a major part in the overall corporate organization.

Our management development review process plays an important role in this area. Each department head makes an annual presentation to the three general executives and myself, acting as a management development review committee, each year. Out of these meetings comes the identification of organizational and personnel problems, but it remains the responsibility of the department head to develop his proposals for meeting the specified needs.

An executive of an oil and gas company explained his company's approach as follows:

Task determination and responsibility relationships are functions of the various department heads in our oil operations and are handled by independent management in our wholly owned subsidiaries. Project planning, as distinct from organization planning, involves our economic and planning department in coordination with operating department heads. Top management and our all-internal board of directors are involved in project and budget approvals.

In summary, most companies that have no organization departments because of their size, decentralized structure, or line-staff ideology reported that their line managers are expected to solve their own organization-planning problems without staff consulting advice inside the company.

### COMPANIES WITH COMBINED DEPARTMENTS

Fifty-nine participating firms (44 industrial and 15 nonindustrial) combine organization planning and development with other functions to form one department. When firms are small, the organization planning and development function usually seems to be performed by the president, possibly with the aid of an assistant. As companies grow in size, organization work is performed by a department as a part-time activity, usually supplemented by outside consultants. With increased growth, full-time organization analysts become part of the department staff. As the job grows still larger and more important, the organization section is separated to report to the president or vice-president.

This is the way most organization departments develop. However, another way is creation by the company president when he sees the need.

The organization function may be combined with others in many ways. Carlos Efferson conducted research in the mid-1950s and found the following diverse conditions and practices in the various companies he studied:

- Organization planning was part of industrial engineering.
- Industrial engineering was part of organization planning.
- Organization planning was part of industrial relations.
- Industrial relations was part of organization planning.
- Organization planning was largely operations control.
- Organization planning was largely facility planning.
- Organization planning was largely economic forecasting.
- Organization planning reported to finance, operations, marketing, or industrial relations.
- Departments worked primarily on operations research.
- Departments worked primarily on education.
- Departments dealt with charting an ideal organization, and without reference to implementation.
- Departments worked primarily on communications.
- Departments concentrated mostly on high-level personnel changes.
- Departments worked primarily on manpower and cost controls.

These great variations could be explained by two factors: First, the function itself was new, and standard patterns had not yet evolved; second, many departments had taken on various routine tasks that were not strictly organization planning—industrial engineering, salary administration, or management appraisal, for example—because no one else in the company was doing them. Often these fringe activities constituted the major work of the organization-planning department.

Among the organization-planning departments that had a significant impact on their company's progress, two factors existed:

1. The department personnel and their manager had a strong feeling that planning the future shape and form of the company's departments and functions is an activity of crucial importance.

2. The departments were careful to meet the particular needs of the company, using methods natural to its way of doing business, rather than ivory-tower thinking unrelated to the company's requirements for growth and development.[2]

Dr. Efferson believed that the reporting relationship and placement of organization departments would be clarified as the function matured. Since then, developments have occurred in the direction he predicted: the formation of a separate department or a combination of organization and people-related departments such as personnel. Organization planning and development are now seldom joined with industrial engineering, accounting, finance, operations, or marketing.

Three combinations of organization and another function predominate today. Personnel–industrial relations is by far the most likely combination. This is not surprising, however, for organization matters involve human relationships, management development, manpower planning, and other aspects of industrial relations. Some departments include organization and top-level manpower management development—excluding blue collar and white collar activities handled by personnel departments.

The second most prevalent combination involves corporate planning and development. This function deals with future growth and adjustments of the firm to changes in product, economy, and environment. Many firms have placed organization-planning groups in this department so that they will consider how the future will affect the organization structure and top management. These groups often consider the potential impact of mergers and acquisitions, make recommendations, and help absorb the new companies into the firm.

Departments of administration, the third combination, are not all cut from the same cloth. In some firms they seem to be catch-all departments; in others, housekeepers for line departments. Some administration departments seem to be personnel departments renamed after the addition of other functions, such as systems groups, legal departments, public or corporate relations. Others are a combination of financial and legal functions plus some housekeeping services.

According to Dr. Efferson, organization planning and development is often joined with personnel and other departments because staff executives need organization work to do their other jobs well. He said:

> A major reason for personnel's close association with organization is that good personnel men—the ones with initiative and conscientious responsibility—have found that about 80 percent of what are usually considered communication problems is really poor organization. Good communication cannot occur in a poorly organized company. So the personnel men find it natural to get into organization. In the case of corporate planning, good controllers found that they can't do a good job of financial planning until they get some clear ideas about what their company is and what it should be. So they reach out, and the first thing you know they've got corporate business planning.
>
> I think this accounts for a lot of the variation in the combination and construction of organization departments. The good men simply moved in where the vacuums were.

### The Formation of Departments

Organization executives were asked when the organization planning and development function was established in their companies, and who established it. More than half of the companies established the function after 1960. All the smaller firms and a large percentage of the medium-size ones had been created after 1955. Only a few pioneering companies set up organization departments before 1950. A few were established in the early 1950s, and still more in the late 1950s; but most of the growth came in the 1960s. One can only speculate on how much growth will come in the 1970s.

The organization executives were asked whose efforts were responsible for their department's establishment. The responses can shed light on the degree of support the department has received from top management, since sponsorship very often determines the function's role and shapes its future development.

In slightly more than two-thirds (58) of the companies, the president or chairman of the board of directors established the function. In the smaller firms and the nonindustrial companies, an even larger number were established by the president or the chairman. (See Ta-

TABLE 1. *Executives responsible for the establishment of organization function in participating companies.*

|  | Industrial companies ||||||  Non-industrial companies || All companies ||
|---|---|---|---|---|---|---|---|---|---|
|  | Large || Medium size || Small || | | | |
| Executives responsible | No. | Per-cent | No. | Per-cent | No. | Per-cent | No. | Per-cent | No. | Per-cent |
| President or chairman of the board | 20 | 59 | 10 | 59 | 10 | 83 | 20 | 80 | 60 | 68 |
| Vice-president (primarily industrial relations or personnel) | 11 | 32 | 4 | 23 | 0 | — | 3 | 12 | 18 | 20 |
| Director (primary personnel or industrial relations) | 3 | 9 | 3 | 18 | 2 | 17 | 2 | 8 | 10 | 12 |

ble 1.) In three-fourths of the companies, the function was established at the vice-presidential level or above it. This evidence confirms the existence of support by upper echelons and the potential influence of organization planning and development.

Several companies that participated in this study described the conditions under which their organization departments were established, the support the departments received, and how they evolved after its establishment.

*Standard Oil Company of California*

At Standard Oil Company of California, the organization department's emphasis has changed as the company's problems and challenges have changed. The department has served the company's executives by providing analysis and advice regarding the most pressing organization problems at the time.

The organization department of this company was one of the first

—if not the first—in the United States. It was established in 1931 by formalizing a task force that had been created to reduce costs through methods improvements. Initially, it reported to the president, but later and at present, to the chairman of the board and the president. The following summary of the department's evolution was provided by its present department head.

During the depression era, 1931–1941, the purpose of the department was to analyze resource and manpower utilization in the company's lower echelons for the purpose of reducing costs. One of the first major studies performed by the department was an analysis of motor transport activities. This study recommended the creation of the motor transport group and reduced the motor fleet by 1,000 pieces of equipment.

Another early study was one that examined the company's compensation and appraisal system. Since the results disclosed divergent systems of compensation and salary, the department recommended that a job-appraisal and compensation department be established to advise in this area. It was made part of the organization department.

From 1941 to 1946, the department helped reorganize the firm for wartime expansion and better utilization of the womanpower replacing the men who were then serving in the armed forces. The department introduced the use of manning tables as a tool of organization planning.

In the postwar period 1946–1957, Standard Oil Company of California experienced great expansion. Again the department helped the company organize for expansion and for meeting the demand for its products. A special organization challenge involved the creation of new subsidiary companies.

Since 1957 greater pressures of costs have led to renewed emphasis on the utilization of manpower, money, and facilities resources. Increased use of improved methods and automation has resulted in more detailed studies of operations and the elimination of some functions and levels of management.

*Bank of America*

Bank of America was developed by a dynamic entrepreneur. Most decisions were centralized for a number of years, and the organization had a centralized functional structure with strong functional leaders. When a new president was elected, the bank evolved toward professional management; then the firm began to operate with profit centers and a strong control system.

In 1951 organization planning was a function of the controller's department, which kept records and updated organization charts. In 1955 the organization department reported to the president and had become oriented to changing organization methods and systems. In 1958 organization studies were being conducted, and the department's emphasis had shifted from remedial activities to forward planning. The department began to anticipate the demands that would be made on the company five to ten years later, and the methods that the company might use to cope with them in terms of organization and manpower adjustment.

## UniRoyal, Incorporated

In 1958 the president of UniRoyal was about to retire, and George R. Vila was chosen to succeed him. Mr. Vila desired to make some changes in the organization structure of the firm that he was to head, and an organization-planning department was created to help in the transition by advising him and implementing his plans for reorganization. The executive in charge of this department described it as follows:

At UniRoyal, organization planning provides a means of getting the job accomplished in the best way that we can devise to do it, and utilizing the best talent that we have available at the moment in the best way possible. We are a catalyst for organization change. If our departments were left to their own devices, they might simply maintain the status quo rather than organize in keeping with our long-range goals.

We have a large organization, so we are able to experiment and devise many different methods of organization design. Almost any textbook organization design or other type of structure that you can name exists somewhere in our company. And we foster this trend because the one thing that we are trying to avoid is a rigid approach, which was the modus operandi in the past.

If you organize either by copying other firms or by following textbook solutions, and decide that a certain type of organization is best, and then proceed to mold all your decisions to fit this pattern, you have problems. It sounds ridiculous, but

I know of companies that are organizing just this way. Or, failing that, they say, "General Motors is a very successful company; therefore, we will organize the way they do."

Today organization planning at UniRoyal has evolved from aiding in the transition between the two presidents to conducting ongoing organization studies, determining future organization needs of the company, and participating in forward planning.

*The Port of New York Authority*

The Port of New York Authority is a bi-state agency of New York and New Jersey that administers transportation and real estate functions for these states.

Organization work was originally performed in the controller's department as part of accounting procedures. Eventually, it was separated and developed into a combination of organization planning and procedures dealing with minor organization problems. Gradually, the work shifted to more complex, higher-level organization problems. Intradepartmental problems were emphasized less, and interdepartmental organization analysis grew more important. Today organization activities are concentrated at the top level as much as possible.

Harvey Sherman, who manages the function, frequently consults with Austin Tobin, administrator of The Port of New York Authority, regarding such problems as the location of a new organization unit, the division of a large department into smaller ones, the centralization or decentralization of staff services, and other such matters. He describes some of these problems in his book, *It All Depends*.[3]

*Kaiser Aluminum and Chemical Corporation*

During the past two decades, Kaiser has grown rapidly. Between 1947 and 1954, employment of 3,800 and sales of $45 million grew to 16,000 employees and $300 million sales, and plans were made for a 50 percent increase in aluminum capacity by 1960. As a result, organization planning was occurring without a formal department for it.

In 1952 Carlos Efferson, the executive who later was to head the department of organization, was conducting manpower studies. Certain problems arose in manpower planning and executive development, and the executive vice-president suggested that an organization-planning department should be created. The initial goals were to determine the needs of the organization; to help clarify organizational roles; to help resolve boundary disputes between organizational elements; and to help control the direction of the company's rapid growth to some extent. Dr. Efferson spoke as follows of the development of the function at Kaiser:

> My company employed me, originally, to establish a management inventory and development program. The program we put into effect featured organization charts of the future and an inventory of the number and type of management members, including estimates of their potentiality.
>
> The important thing is that we found ourselves working on forecasts of future organization structure, just to determine future executive needs. While doing this, my management and I became more and more conscious of the importance of organization planning for itself and for many uses other than forecasting executive needs.

The first act of the new department head was to spend two months in visits to other organization departments throughout the country. Dr. Efferson interviewed directors in a number of departments and summarized his findings in several articles.[4] He studied the various jobs of the directors and then specified the role he wished to fill at Kaiser. His superiors agreed, and thus the company's organization function was established.

### Implications of Department Formation

One factor appeared to have special importance in the creation of organization departments—change-over in company presidency. Earlier research by the author indicates that such a change provides a favorable climate for organization-department development. Professor Paul Lawrence of Harvard Business School voiced a similar observation:

In my studies, I found that change-over of presidency was a most significant period, when organization planning and development staffs either expanded their influence or were created. They were then vehicles to implement the changes the new chief executives and the staff wanted to implement.

This tendency was also noted for Bank of America, UniRoyal, and many other companies.

Another major opportunity for the creation or expansion of these departments is a major change in the environment; rapid economic growth is a notable force in this respect. Such has been the situation at International Business Machines Corporation.

A few firms reported that, although they do not have an organization planning and development department, they intend to create one. These companies include Ralston Purina Company, American Brands, Incorporated, American Metal Climax Corporation, Texas Instruments, Interchemical Corporation, Midland Ross Corporation, Anchor Hocking Corporation, Joy Manufacturing Company, and Inland Container Corporation. Other firms had only recently set up such a department and for this reason could not answer all the questions asked. (This accounts for some discrepancies in the number of answers.) Again, most firms establishing departments were large rather than small, but no industry differences were found. Also, firms that experience rapid change—increased complexity or major management shifts, for example—are the most likely to establish organization departments.

## The Roles of Departments

In complex organizations, the role of staff departments such as organization planning and development is largely determined by their relationships with various executives and groups in the company. Logically, the department's most important relations are with the executive to whom the department head reports, the department's clients, and others involved in or affected by its activities. Rarely can organization departments determine structures and relationships by a simple request for approval. Other elements of the corporation are usually concerned formally in the organization planning and development process.

## Reporting Relationships

The title of the department head gives some indication of the relationship between the department and the corporation's decision makers. Over half (60) of 115 participating companies have a vice-president in charge of the function and approximately one-fourth (29 firms) have directors in charge. Nineteen percent (22 companies) have managers as heads of their organization departments, and a few have an assistant to the president in this position. (See Table 2.)

TABLE 2. *Titles of department heads in participating companies.*

|  | Industrial companies | | | |
|---|---|---|---|---|
| Titles | Large | Medium size | Small | All industrials |
| Vice-president | 16 | 11 | 14 | 41 |
| Director | 12 | 7 | 5 | 24 |
| Manager | 7 | 3 | 5 | 15 |
| Assistant to the president | 1 | 2 | 1 | 4 |
| Totals | 36 | 23 | 25 | 84 |

|  | Nonindustrial companies | | | | All non-industrials |
|---|---|---|---|---|---|
|  | Financial | Merchandising | Transportation | Utilities |  |
| Vice-president | 13 | 3 | 1 | 2 | 19 |
| Director | 1 | 2 | 1 | 1 | 5 |
| Manager | 1 | 2 | 2 | 2 | 7 |
| Totals | 15 | 7 | 4 | 5 | 31 |

When these findings are compared with Professor Bailey's, there appears to be an increase in the number of vice-presidents in charge of the function.[5]

Another, and sometimes better, indicator of influence is the reporting relationship of the department head. Three-fourths (86) of the organization department heads report to the president or chairman of the board. More than 20 percent report to a vice-president, or the second level of management. Thus, in 95 percent of these companies, organization departments have an opportunity to significantly influence management decisions at the top level. (See Table 3.)

TABLE 3. *Reporting relationships of department heads in participating companies.*

|  | Industrial companies ||||||| Nonindustrial companies || All companies ||
|  | Large firms || Medium-size firms || Smaller firms |||||||
| Levels reported to | No. | Per-cent | No. | Per-cent | No. | Per-cent | No. | Per-cent | No. | Per-cent |
| --- | --- | --- | --- | --- | --- | --- | --- | --- | --- | --- |
| First (chairman of board or president) | 21 | 60 | 18 | 81 | 23 | 85 | 24 | 75 | 86 | 74 |
| Second (vice-president) | 10 | 28 | 3 | 14 | 4 | 15 | 8 | 25 | 25 | 21 |
| Third (director— e.g., personnel) | 5 | 12 | 1 | 5 | 0 | 0 | 0 | 0 | 6 | 5 |
| Totals | 36 | 100 | 22 | 100 | 27 | 100 | 32 | 100 | 117 | 100 |

Of the six executives reporting to the third level, three report to division heads because their companies have decentralized most of the staff and located them in divisions. They too, probably, would have an opportunity to significantly influence management decisions in their divisions.

What about other relationships within the firm? If there is an organization department, does this preclude others from working on organization problems? This study found that the larger the company, the less likely it is that other staffs (such as personnel departments), outside consultants, or line executives are involved in organization. The smaller the company, the more likely it is to use line executives to solve such problems. Medium-size companies most frequently use committees.

In addition, the most important individuals involved with the organization department on organization matters are the top line executives. Vice-presidents in charge of product divisions provide an example: These executives frequently bring in the organization department to study problems and make recommendations.

Organization executives were asked which other individuals or groups spend the most time on organization activities. They indicated that committees and outside consultants are seldom a primary source of organization assistance. In many of the participating companies, the organization department and its staff are either "on their own" or they work with the line executives. Line executives on various levels handle about a third of the companies' organization problems themselves, without consulting the department.

Corporate organization decisions are usually made by top management alone, with organization specialists helping implement these decisions. When organization specialists work with divisional line executives, they are coping with divisional organization problems that they try to resolve within the corporate guidelines. As an executive of a large electronics firm explained it: "Divisional line executives work on problems generally similar to corporate problems in nature, but only on those problems affecting the operations of their own division."

An executive of another large firm said that its divisional line executives are involved with the entire spectrum of organization activities, but within their division or subsidiary.

In a large metal-products company, divisional line executives are concerned with organizational implications of operating problems and short-term organization plans. By contrast, a large textile company's organization specialist reported: "The divisional line executives are involved with aligning their organizational patterns and their people toward their objectives, and fostering individual development activities."

## Types of Roles

Effective staff executives are experts at delicately balancing the multiple roles they must play to accomplish their goals. The most important of these roles are listed by Leonard Sayles in *Managerial Behavior:*

*Advisory:* furnishing advice on organization problems when requested by line executives.

*Service:* performing activities for the corporation that divisions could do themselves, such as maintaining manuals, drawing charts, running routine surveys.

*Auditing:* supervising the extent to which line departments comply with corporate policies regarding organization and organization changes.

*Stabilization:* obtaining approval of staff groups before making changes in organization structure.

*Innovation:* constantly surveying the organization to look for trouble spots and inefficiencies, and suggesting to appropriate executives the availability of their services for improving the organization.[6]

The behavioral requirements of each of these roles have been described in detail by the same author.[7]

Much has been written about the line-staff conflict.[8] But there has been little discussion of intrarole conflict. A role that includes aspects of auditing and stabilizing, and advising and innovating, is almost impossible to handle effectively. The client (the line executive) is never sure whether the organization specialist is there to help, or to check; the client therefore is reluctant to reveal his real problems, since they may be reported back as his inadequacies.

If it is necessary for a staff function to include audit, it should be clearly separated organizationally so that both functions can lead to effective results.

Today's organization specialists spend considerable time informing executives about the relatively sophisticated level of organization planning and development. Many executives would not hesitate to call the legal department for information regarding an antitrust suit but are reluctant to ask for help in the area of organization. "After all," they reason, "isn't every executive supposed to know how to organize?"

For these reasons it is especially important that organization specialists carefully define their various roles. If the auditing–stabilization role is too dominant, line executives may assume that the specialist is trying to check up on his activities rather than helping him.

## Responsibilities

Organization executives were asked how their responsibilities differ from those of others responsible for organization. Most of them replied in one or two ways:

1. Organization executives make decisions at policy level, while line executives are responsible for execution at their own level.

2. Organization executives only provide advice; line executives make organization decisions based on this advice.

A typical example of the first response is—

At this time my responsibility is more toward the corporate needs, and the line groups' responsibility is rather toward their particular areas. (Large consumer-products company)

The line executives are responsible for all organization matters below the level at which decision making is centralized. (Large automobile firm)

The organization executive of one large manufacturing firm reported a different division of responsibilities: "The scope of line organization-development responsibilities is limited to assigned divisions, departments, and other units, whereas my responsibilities are companywide. Also, they have authority to act, whereas I provide advice and assistance as well as control."

The second type of response included these examples:

The line managers are authorized to make manpower or organization changes; we advise, present alternatives, provide information, keep records. (Large oil company)

They implement the plans and programs we develop. (Medium-size metals firm)

They have line responsibility for results. We provide advice, consultation, and research. (Mining company)

But authority can go both ways. An executive in a medium-size consumer goods company stated: "We work closely with line people on all levels. They approve our organization proposals. We make recommendations regarding theirs."

At the research seminar, two organization specialists discussed their role relationships in detail. Carlos Efferson of Kaiser described his role as advisory or inside consultant.

We operate much more on the service or captive-consultant basis than on the audit or control basis. First of all, I work for the president. One might say that I provide organizational control, in the sense that he asks my advice; I give him my recommendations; and if he accepts them and makes a line decision, control is being exercised. But I think the important point is that a staff department receives a yes-or-no decision from the president on certain things. In this case, it doesn't serve on a control basis.

Some organization-planning departments are very largely audit-oriented—and very powerful. For example, in one large oil company the organization department goes into division operations and studies them thoroughly, working with and through the division. But the head of the division knows that what this group recommends has the weight of the president behind it and is, in effect, a presidential audit. After the group has reached its conclusions, the manager of the division just studied goes to the president with the conclusions and his plans for change. The organization group seldom has to give the manager orders by way of the president, because the manager goes along with the group's decisions, or he convinces the organization-department people that they are wrong. Still, the whole procedure amounts to an audit, and everybody knows this.

Dr. Efferson pointed out that organization specialists often have a more confidential role.

Top managers often end up discussing subjects with organization men that are highly confidential and have little if anything to do with organization. This is mainly because even top managers have to talk to somebody. All the managers can do when they get an urge to discuss such things is to hope the organization man keeps quiet.

One organization-development specialist complained that he was the "loneliest man in town." The corporate headquarters was in a small town, and the organization man knew a good deal about the company organization changes that affected people's careers. He found he did not dare discuss these matters with anyone, even his physician; for, in at least one case, the physician had another patient who wanted the doctor to find out certain things for him. The organization specialist said, "I never talk about my work. Conversation must be steered to neutral ground—football, or the weather."

James H. Davis of Alcoa believes that the effective organization specialist can adapt easily to various situations and to executives who are his clients. He said:

The character of our work and the balance of the workload—in terms of more fundamental, less quick pay-out stuff, continues to change. We avoid a confrontation if we possibly can. We state our position and defend it, but don't impose it on a man if we can help it. After all, we're not running the department. If the other man doesn't follow our advice and falls on his face, we let him. Next time he'll be ready to listen. And if he succeeds by going against our advice, then we've learned something—our solution wasn't the best one. We try to avoid confronting a man or hauling him up to his boss. That's an instance where you may lose, even if you win.

Mr. Davis reinforced this point by discussing a situation that required distinguishing between the counseling and auditing roles.

*Organization Departments and Organization Executives* 43

In one of our works locations, the division manager sent us in to work on an organization problem. The works manager's boss said that he could not make organizational changes until I "approved" them. The boss literally put me between himself and his subordinate. To me, this was a very unsatisfactory role to give to someone who's trying to be counselor. Obviously, the works manager has little or no choice; he'll agree with whatever I say if he wants to accomplish anything. This is an impossible role for an adviser.

There's an audit element that I've identified in our company, too. We believe some things ought to be done a certain way because they seem to meet the company's objectives. Perhaps we immodestly think we can sense what these objectives are, better than the boss who's running one little part of the business. But we've also found that if those controls are conspicuous, we lose our position as a consultant. So we've established controls in an organization-analysis department and put them in another department for administration and audit. We control through one part of our work—we generate descriptions of jobs, and evaluate the jobs and establish the grade of the job. And we turn this over to the salary administration department to administer. They handle salary problems, promotional increases, and this sort of thing.

## Departmental Size and Composition

Another important dimension of organization departments is size. Previous studies have indicated that organization departments have relatively small staffs. Among the reasons given for the small size were the following:

- The nature of the work requires only a few full-time staff members. When the work is heavy, companies can temporarily supplement the staff with a task force of executives or with outside consultants.
- Since the staff is concerned with efficiency, it should be a small, elite group who resisted Parkinson's law and avoided expansion.[9]

To determine whether most companies have small organization staffs, participants were asked to indicate the number of professionals, secretaries, and clerks in their departments. If the department had several functions, participants were asked to state the number of employees who worked only on organization planning and development activities.

Forty-four percent (24) of 54 large industrial firms have three or fewer professional personnel who concentrate on organization work only. But 56 percent (30) have four or more professionals performing organization activities. Almost three-fourths (37) of these companies have three or fewer clerical-support personnel for the professionals. Most of these employees work only on organization matters.

As expected, small and medium-size firms tend to have smaller organization departments; approximately three-fourths of them employ three professionals or fewer. Most participating companies have fewer than seven professionals in their organization departments. (See Table 4.)

TABLE 4. *Number of professionals and clerical personnel in organization departments of participating companies, industrial and nonindustrial.*

| No. of personnel | No. of companies with professionals in the department | No. of professionals working on organization development alone | No. of clerical workers in department | No. of clerical workers working only on organization development |
|---|---|---|---|---|
| *Large companies* | | | | |
| 3 or fewer | 24 | 24 | 37 | 32 |
| 4 to 6 | 11 | 7 | 7 | 1 |
| 7 to 10 | 9 | 5 | 0 | 0 |
| 11 to 15 | 5 | 0 | 4 | 0 |
| More than 15 | 5 | 0 | 2 | 0 |
| Totals | 54 | 36 | 50 | 33 |
| *Medium-size companies* | | | | |
| 3 or fewer | 9 | 4 | 11 | 4 |
| 4 to 6 | 3 | 1 | 0 | 0 |
| More than 6 | 0 | 0 | 1* | 0 |
| Totals | 12 | 5 | 12 | 4 |
| *Smaller companies* | | | | |
| 3 or fewer | 4 | 3 | 4 | 2 |
| 4 to 6 | 2 | 0 | 1 | 0 |
| More than 6 | 1 | 0 | 1* | 0 |
| Totals | 7 | 3 | 6 | 2 |
| Grand Totals | 73 | 44 | 68 | 39 |

* Company organization department has more than 15 professionals and clerical workers.

In general, the larger the department, the more likely it is that the professionals and clerical personnel spend their time on both organization and other activities; and the smaller the department, the more likely they are to be full-time organization specialists.

## Organization Executives

A previous study conducted by the author on the characteristics of organization executives disclosed that 42 percent of them had graduate degrees (primarily at the master's level), 45 percent had bachelor's degrees, 5 percent had some college education, and 17 percent had attended or graduated from high school. A profile of their business careers showed that the average director had 19 years of business experience and had held approximately four positions in three functions, with three companies. Most of their experience (90 percent) was in staff positions, usually in personnel or corporate-planning positions.[10]

Similar data were gathered from 86 executives responding to the staff executive's questionnaire. More than four-fifths (72) had bachelor's degrees; of these one-third (24) had obtained a master's degree in addition. A large number of the executives had studied business administration or engineering. Some of the executives in larger manufacturing companies were lawyers with an industrial relations background. Some insurance and banking firms also had lawyers in organization jobs.

Almost two-thirds (64 percent, 57) of 89 executives had been in their jobs for three years or less. Only 20 percent (18) had been in their jobs more than six years. However, 55 percent (49) had been doing organization work more than six years. A large number of men were newcomers; about one-third (31) had less than three years' experience in the field. No particular pattern of employment within the company was apparent.

Several organization-department executives provided some insight into the staffing and development practices of their firms. Harvey Sherman of The Port of New York Authority contends that the best organization specialists have ability in handling both details and concepts.

The kind of person I look for is schizophrenic; he's got to be good at both concepts and detail. That is, he ought to have A's in philosophy and A's in accounting. He should be an idealist who believes that everything can be improved. He ought to be highly critical, but trusted by people. He ought to be creative and original, but sound. These characteristics are contradictory, yet I look for a person with these combinations of attributes.

We have men with all kinds of backgrounds—public and private administration, line and staff experience. My department has 25 professionals, of whom about one-third spend all or most of their time on organization. In a sense, I assign my people to whatever projects there are at the time, according to their ability and background. But they don't specialize in any formal way. The only way they specialize is informally, by client department. Within that framework I want the greatest flexibility possible. So I've got one lawyer, one structural engineer, one industrial engineer, and a Ph.D. economist. We have great variety, although the largest proportion of our people have business and public administration background.

James H. Davis of Alcoa explained how his department is partly operational, partly in training. He said:

My department contains eight men. The younger men work on short-run and more expedient projects. The senior executives concentrate on long-run projects. One of our operating practices is that half of my organization is made up of men loaned from other parts of the company. I turn over half of my entire staff roughly every 15 months. These men are nominated by their managements to work for us. We train them in our skills and techniques, and they usually leave to be promoted. This pattern is deliberately planned to put into key spots and broaden people who are sensitive to organization so they can handle organization problems as line executives.

At present, I have one assistant who was an assistant works manager, one who was a quality assurance man (an inspector and metallurgist), one who was a production manager, one who is a smelting expert, one who is an electrical engineer from the construction division, one who was an industrial engineer, and one who came from a sales office. I'm an industrial engineer, myself.

Our first goal is to get a mix of disciplines. Of all our people, temporary and permanent alike, about a third have MBA's or master's degrees in another field. This was not deliberately planned; it just seems that men with this type of education have exhibited interest in their careers that makes them outstanding as candidates. But one of our men was not a college graduate, and he proved quite effective.

We bring in men when they are between 35 and 50 years old. Our experience has been that, under 35, the man has too little exposure at top levels or cannot deal effectively with high-level contacts. After 50, being assigned to this environment for 15 to 18 months is too much jumping around for him; also, if he is a really good man, he's already in a key spot and we can't benefit him enough.

We've really had very good luck with everything under the sun. We've put a great deal of stress on teaching the men organization techniques and requiring them to expose their logic to the other seven men. And we learn from each other in this regard.

Concerning the assignments of these organization specialists, Mr. Davis said:

I spend most of my time on top-level organization problems. My chief lieutenants (who are permanent members of the department) spend some of their time on top-level assignments, and a bigger part on the middle level. Our analysts spend their time on the middle and lower levels. When a junior man comes in, he works entirely on lower- or foreman-level problems, such as redesigning a department in a plant. Job assignments are graded; the men work on problems with different degrees of sophistication.

## Satisfaction in the Job

An attempt was made in this study to determine the degree of satisfaction experienced by the directors in their jobs. In general, the directors indicated that they are not satisfied with their positions. They are especially dissatisfied with what they consider lack of understanding of organization work on the part of management. Their malcontent is intensified by the low rate of acceptance of their suggestions by line management.

This complaint is somewhat ironic, considering that many executives seemed pleased with the extent of their contacts with management. Although they indicated that the outcome of these contacts is often disappointing, the *number* of contacts is evidently more than acceptable.

Another source of dissatisfaction is the type of problems on which they work: The executives believe that they often receive the wrong problems to study. A number of them expressed only moderate satisfaction or even dissatisfaction with management's understanding of their role. However, many were satisfied with management's acceptance of their suggestions. Relations between management and the organization department appear to be a major problem, although many directors believe that top management gives them adequate support. The problem seems to be less severe in medium-size companies than in large and small firms.

*The President's Evaluation*

One way to determine the extent to which top management actually does understand the role of a department head is to ask company presidents for their evaluation of their organization executives' performance.

In this survey the presidents reported that their organization executives performed best in these areas: understanding top management's role; working with management; and making sound recommendations.

The areas rated lowest in performance by the presidents were as follows: solving operating problems; setting priorities for organization workload; and influencing top management.

The presidents seemed moderately satisfied with the executives' ability to solve organizational problems and their ability to help others solve them.

Thus, not only do organization executives feel that they are not influencing top management (though they are able to obtain top management's support); in addition, top managers agree that the executives are not influential. This may help explain why the problems to which executives are assigned are not the ones they feel they should be handling.

This is probably the fate of most new functions in firms: Because management has done the job without the department before, the line managers must be convinced that the function is really necessary. During their early days, personnel relations, marketing research, and operations research no doubt encountered similar resistance.

Dalton E. McFarland, in his surveys of the personnel function,[11] found that presidents believed more work should be done in organization planning. However, the presidents' desires were not fulfilled because personnel directors saw little need for this type of work. If presidents want more work accomplished in the function but are not overly positive in their evaluation of the department's performance, obviously the department heads need to do a better job in selling their function and themselves to top management. Only by building a history of successful accomplishment can the department create a demand for the use of the department's capabilities. Most successful departments achieved their success the hard way—by gaining the confidence of top management, which then entrusted the organization planners with the types of problems that are real challenges.

## References

1. Joseph Bailey, "Organization Planning: Whose Responsibility?" *Academy of Management Journal*, Vol. 7 (June 1964), pp. 96–108.

2. Reported in Carlos Efferson, "Some Basic Considerations in Organization Planning," *Academy of Management Journal*, Vol. 2 (April 1959), p. 31.

3. Harvey Sherman, *It All Depends* (University of Alabama Press, 1969).

4. For a report of these findings, see Carlos Efferson, "Organization Planning for Management Growth," *Management Record*, Vol. 20 (April 1958), p. 134.

5. Bailey, op. cit.

6. Leonard Sayles, *Managerial Behavior* (New York: McGraw-Hill, 1964), pp. 76–110.

7. Ibid.

8. For an excellent treatment of this significant problem by an outstanding author, see Melville Dalton, "Changing Staff-Line Relationships," *Personnel Administration* (March 1966), p. 3.

9. "Parkinson's law," propounded by British writer C. Northcote Parkinson, states that "work expands to fill the time available to complete it." [*Parkinson's Law, or the Pursuit of Progress* (London: John Murray, 1958), p. 4.]

10. William F. Glueck, "Directors of Departments of Organization: Their Educational Achievement and Career Patterns," *MSU Business Topics* (Winter 1969), pp. 44–54.

11. Dalton E. McFarland, *Company Officers Assess the Personnel Function*, AMA Research Study 79 (1967).

# 3. Purposes and Objectives of the Function

Most executives would agree that the purposes and goals of an organization have a strong impact on its achievements. Business organizations are totally aware that their firms are profit-oriented and that profit is one of the major goals of the business. For service-oriented organizations, goals are more difficult to specify. If, for example, a hospital administrator is asked to name the goals of his organization, he is likely to mention first the provision of effective patient care and other services to the sick. Although some authorities believe that there is increasing overlap between the private sector, the public sector, and the not-for-profit sector of our economy, the differences in their goals are still great. There is little question that consumer-goods manufacturers are more profit-oriented than hospitals, and that the latter are more service-oriented than manufacturers.

Both "goal" and "objective" can be defined as "a desired state of affairs that an organization attempts to realize."[1] On another level, a goal can be viewed as a constraint on behavior in decision making.[2] Thus, once a hospital chooses a goal of patient-care and service, it may have difficulty in legitimating a profit-oriented goal.

Goals serve the function of defining the purposes of the organization in a complex environment. They become the criteria by which we relate diverse tasks and coordinate activities. They also direct the attention of employees to work behavior and can become the basis of standards for evaluating the performance of an organization. Goals can be arrived at through historical precedent, but frequently are in fact the results of compromise and discussion among the relevant decision makers in the organization.[3]

Just as goals chosen or bargained for influence the behavior of the organization, goals and subgoals influence activities in the subparts, and relations between the subpart and the whole organization. Thus the stated goals of organization departments influence what these departments do or try to do. Since corporate presidents play a vital role in shaping such departments, their views of goals, purposes, and activities provide some insights about the growth of the organization function.

### Goals Perceived by Presidents

Presidents of participating companies were asked to specify the primary objectives of organization planning and development in their firms. The following classifications of goals are representative of their responses:

1. The goals relate to the company's goals and its long-range planning and policy decisions.
2. The goals are the same or similar to the personnel department's goals.
3. The primary goals refer to the development of an efficient organization structure.
4. The goals are an integration of goals 2 and 3.
5. The goals are to perform organization activities for the company.

Detailed goal statements provided by presidents are provided for each of these categories.

### Goals Relating to Company Goals

Departmental goals relating to company goals had three patterns: (1) the goals are the same as the goals of the company—inseparable; (2) the goals are to contribute to the goal achievements of the company; (3) the goals are to contribute to the company goals by being a part of the total planning or business policy planning function of the company.

Several presidents simply equated the department's goals with company goals and did not differentiate between them. Some typical statements of goals were as follows:

To obtain the highest return on the stockholders' equity. (Equipment manufacturer)

To increase company earnings. (Oil company)

To keep the company moving ahead of competition; to introduce new products and new and better methods of cost control; to find new sales methods and techniques. (Meat packer)

To fulfill the corporate objectives of return on investment and growth. (A.O. Smith Corporation)

The second variation of this goal is more means than end; it rests on the premise that organization departments exist to further corporate goals. Specifically, it sees organization planning and development contributing to the attainment of corporate goals or making effective use of corporate resources. However, the presidents did not explain how this was done. Typical of the statements of goals relating to effectiveness and utilization of company resources were these:

To achieve greater effectiveness and efficiency in working toward corporate goals. (Electric utility)

To organize the company's resources to most effectively meet the company's objectives. (Steel company)

To utilize the corporate resources properly. (Sperry Rand Corporation)

To maximize the effective utilization of corporate resources in meeting the needs of constantly changing environments. (National Cash Register)

To maximize the profit of the company by making sure that our plans are adequate for the future needs of the company and that we have the people to carry them out. (Brunswick Corporation)

This type of statement was the response of a number of presidents. Other representative statements referred to profits and growth —for example, the following:

To assure both short- and long-term profitable growth. (Union Bank)

To increase the profitable growth of the corporation. (Crompton and Knowles Corporation)

To enable the company to grow and continue to maintain or improve profit percentage. (Aircraft manufacturer)

*Purposes and Objectives of the Function* 53

The third type of goal statements given by the presidents indicated that the organization goals are related to the goals of long-range planning, corporate planning, or business policy planning: That is, they are either the same as or similar to the planning goals. Typical responses included the following:

To evolve an organization best suited to achieve our objectives and strategy as defined in the long-range corporate objectives and strategy plan. (Control Data)

To appraise the future, its problems and opportunities, and to determine the quantity and quality of personnel and capital needed to realize reasonable predetermined objectives. (Bank)

To create a systematic, regular procedure for setting goals, for auditing progress toward goals, and for adequate communication measures to keep all company organizations informed about the progress that has been made in other organizations. (Lukens Steel Corporation)

To draw up short-range and long-range plans for the corporation in consultation with top management and the appropriate operating and staff groups. Also, to assume primary responsibility for the implementation of long-range planning in areas of acquisitions and mergers. (Chemical company)

Some variations of this goal were also provided:

To identify problems and basic trends affecting our business; to devise plans to maximize our opportunities for profitable growth. (Girard Trust Bank)

To determine what our business is and should be, and how best to accomplish sales and profit growth objectives. (Anchor Hocking)

To establish long-range objectives and goals; then to establish gap between goals and present achievement. (Steel company)

To keep long-range and short-range problems in proper perspective without losing sight of either type. (Weyerhaeuser company)

Thus no subgoals are established for departments in these companies, since the presidents link the departments closely with corporate plans and objectives.

*Goals Oriented to Personnel Function*

The presidents of some companies see few differences between the goals of personnel and those of organization. Their statements on the subject had two variations: first, the frequently listed goals or functions of personnel administration (selection, promotion, training, and other personnel activities); second, maximizing the use of human resources.

Trying to separate duties into mutually agreed-upon functions is a difficult and perhaps endless process; thus it is natural that some presidents mentioned activities that most personnel specialists would claim as their own. But this also suggests that these presidents think of organization planning and development as a new name for personnel, or that in these companies organization planning and development really is a personnel function. In some firms it is equivalent to management development or to the training and development of personnel, as indicated by the following examples:

To try to develop manpower to run a growing company and to enable people to achieve personal satisfaction, to the extent of their talents. (Large food-retailing company)

To achieve results based on objectives by having well-trained manpower available. (Retailer)

To promote the development of personal initiative and commitment and to develop and improve products and profit. (Copper company)

Other presidents closely identify the goals of organization departments with motivating company employees. For example:

To motivate and increase the competence of the employees, to provide for growth, and to provide for change in individuals. (Large manufacturer)

To evaluate all persons, to encourage them, and to give them responsibility. (Textile company)

To involve all the necessary people in our company's objectives. (Equipment manufacturer)

Other presidents seem to equate the organization function's goals with the effective placement of employees. These presidents typically stated goals as follows:

To get the best people we can into the key jobs; to assure that they continue to be effective and properly motivated; to acquire and develop high-potential people, both to do a better job of managing our existing business and for future growth. (Cabot Corporation)

## Purposes and Objectives of the Function

To place the most qualified people in all positions and provide each with all the available tools to effect the best utilization of human and financial resources so as to promote improvement in all areas compatible with established goals. (Amphenol Corporation)

Some presidents believe that the goals of organization planning and development are closely tied to the staffing function. Participants provided these examples:

To promote the continuing, full utilization of our human resources; to have people ready for key positions as needed; to communicate corporate objective and philosophy to our employees, our shareholders, and the public. (Boise Cascade Corporation)

To provide growth in numbers and in competence, in line with the planned growth of our company. (Packing company)

To have capable personnel available to carry out the corporate objectives. (Kelsey Hayes company)

To provide capable, qualified employee candidates to the best staff organization positions made available by acquisition and diversification. (Comet Rice Mills)

To assure adequate staffing at all levels of management. (Life insurance company)

Other presidents identified the goals of organization planning and development by listing one or several activities or functions usually performed by personnel departments.

To develop the existing staff for greater responsibility and the selection and training of personnel for the future. (Machinery manufacturer)

To attract, retain, and develop sufficient management talent to meet the challenges of today's and tomorrow's business environment. (General Time Corporation)

To maintain an adequate supply of happy and effective personnel to operate the current business at a fair return to stockholders; to be able to expand the business, either on plan or on opportunity; to insure healthy corporate continuity by continuously assessing and evaluating the company's human resources. (Remington Arms Company)

To establish results-oriented position guides and standards of performance; to maintain a manpower inventory audit reflecting managerial skills and development needs; and to create an employee reserve of capable, qualified candidates to best staff organization positions. (Large manufacturer)

Probably the most frequent goal relating to these functions concerns the promotion, motivation, and development of managers or management teams. This is not surprising, since many organization-development departments evolved from a merging of organization planning, which is oriented to structural change and analysis, with management development. However, these presidents see organization development as management development, with no relation to organization analysis. Typical examples include the following goals:

To strengthen management teams and build for the future. (Central National Bank of Cleveland)

To provide necessary management talent at all levels to carry out company growth plans and improve management efficiency. (Chemical processor)

To assist line and staff in planning which will insure continuity of excellent management, and to provide consulting services on techniques of identifying and developing management potential and improving effectiveness of management teams. (St. Regis Paper Company)

To make sure there is trained management available for growth needs as well as turnover. (Copper Range Company)

Other presidents expressed a similar orientation, but they concentrated on management development.

To train and develop management personnel, and plan for adequate management manpower. (Electric utility)

To locate, train, and develop managers and executives to assure continued growth of the company. (White Motor Corporation)

To develop an aggressive cost-, market-, and profit-conscious executive group and give recognition to internal growth and promotion, and at the same time infuse sufficient outside talent to keep the organization alive and vital. (Island Creek Coal Company)

To upgrade the strength of management organization. (The Stanley Works)

To develop a stronger sense of responsibility, especially for profit, and a more professional approach to management in our managers. (Consolidated Papers)

One final variation of this type of goal is the frequently quoted objective of personnel: to maximize the use of human resources, and to increase the satisfaction of the company's employees. This goal tends to be listed for organization-development approaches even though it does not specify that organization is to serve as a means to its achievement. Some examples of such goals, which are applicable to both personnel departments and organization-development departments, are the following:

To best utilize the talents and abilities of our people to achieve maximum efficiency in operation, including sales and the development and training of new people. (Dura Corporation)

To achieve effective, efficient use of available manpower. (Texas City Refining Corporation)

To achieve operating objectives with a minimum number of employees in all categories of employment. (Major airline)

To keep the company an aggressive contender in its field by providing facilities, and to keep manpower at the proper level. (Olympia Brewing Company)

To provide an effective and efficient means to the realization of company goals by providing an effective pattern of personnel utilization. (George A. Hormel and Company)

## Organization-Planning Goals

Some company presidents indicated that the primary goal of organization departments is the creation of an effective and efficient organization structure for the corporation. They believe that analyzing and improving this structure enables the company to run more effectively. Goal statements by some of the presidents illustrate this point.

To develop an organization structure most effective in meeting corporate goals and objectives. [Standard Oil Company (Indiana)]

To assist in the attainment of corporate objectives by appraising the organization structure in the light of changed internal and external conditions and assuring that organizational revisions required to meet these changed conditions are accomplished, and in an orderly manner. (Oil company)

To find a structure within which the company's affairs can be conducted with a maximum of impact and a minimum of internal friction. (Large conglomerate)

To keep the organization structure properly adapted to current market and operating conditions, and to prepare the organization to take advantage of future industry trends, product changes, and market developments. (Central National Bank)

In some cases the statements of the presidents not only indicated that the goal was to analyze and develop the organization structure but also specified the anticipated results. For example:

To develop an organization structure which will provide maximum efficiency; clear downward communication of management objectives; upward communication of operating needs; minimum supervision required for adequate control. (Bank of America)

To define the responsibility and authority of managers, and to provide a corporate structure that permits a free exercise of that responsibility. To establish the necessary limitations of authority and controls. (National Homes Corporation)

To distribute the workload so that each executive and department has a well-defined area of responsibility and authority, leading to the successful attainment of corporate goals and objectives. (Eastern Airlines)

To provide for orderly progression of organization, in accordance with the company's planned rate of growth, so as to provide all the necessary elements at the right time and in the right place. (Conglomerate)

To develop an effective chain of command, effective staff work, effective communifications flow, and effective guidance and control of the organization. (Brewing company)

Some presidents defined their organization department goals by listing some of the duties or responsibilities of the departments. For example:

To provide professional services in evaluating and improving organization structure; to assist in making necessary changes; and to maintain a reasonable degree of uniformity and consistency within the company organization. (Large retailer)

To control employment costs; to improve the effectiveness of the organization and the total performance; to predict organization changes; and to provide consistency of application of accepted policies. (Major steel corporation)

Finally, some company presidents listed a specific company structural change:

To return to centralized-management principle. (Calumet and Hecla Corporation)

To establish a decentralized organization structure to maximize unit-profit responsibility, and yet to maintain adequate corporate guidance and control. (Building materials manufacturer)

To encourage organizational parallelism between the corporation and the divisions. (Lockheed)

*Purposes and Objectives of the Function* 59

## Organization-Development Goals

Departments that are oriented to organization development attempt to integrate the goals and activities of the organization-planning/structural activities and certain management development/personnel activities. Participating presidents expressed these goals in three slightly different ways: first, as organization-development goals; second, as organization-development goals that concentrate on building an effective organization; and third, as organization-development goals that emphasize building an effective organization capable of growing and adapting in a changing world.

Some presidents provided goals concerned with effective organization structure and effective people staffing it. Examples of these goal statements include:

To provide skills and capabilities required to support our growth plans. To motivate key personnel to optimum performance. To develop effective, efficient organization structure for our business. (Manufacturing company)

To create a smoothly working organization in which responsibilities and accountabilties are defined and known, with competent, well-trained individuals functioning together as a team. (Massachusetts Mutual Life Insurance Company)

To establish objectives, mold the organization so that objectives may be reached, develop the leaders necessary to accomplish the objectives, and instill a system of controls to check on progress made in meeting the objectives. (Recreation equipment manufacturer)

To provide for smooth management continuity, organization structures that facilitate growth, effective deployment of managerial talent, and continual improvement of organization and managerial strength. (Non-durable-products company)

To improve work flow of organization; to improve accuracy of job performance evaluation; develop future key executives; and strengthen communications. (Royal Crown Cola Company)

Other examples of this set of goals include the following:

To provide employees with the organization, environment, and a portion of the incentives necessary to maintain their long-range cooperation, enthusiasm, and loyalty. (Gerber Products Company)

To develop organization attitudes, relationships, and objectives of the company which will provide challenge and opportunity for growth and advancement of key personnel. (Sun Chemical Company)

To provide an organizational framework within which the basic responsibilities for operating and developing the business are fully assigned, people can work together effectively, and results can be evaluated in terms of personal effectiveness. (Glass company)

To create and review corporate organization structure toward the goal of obtaining the most efficient and clearly defined lines of responsibility possible, and to identify and develop managerial talent. (Airline)

To have well-trained people in all positions and to have an effective, efficient organization. (Panhandle Eastern Pipe Line Company)

Other presidents expressed similar goals with somewhat less detail:

To improve organizational structure and aid in long-range manpower planning. (Lukens Steel)

To give closer attention to top-level manpower and organization planning and appraisal. [Standard Oil Company (Ohio)]

To achieve satisfactory operating results, and make best use of talents of people; to keep organization structure in tune with changing conditions. (Bankers Life and Casualty Company)

A few presidents emphasized that their ultimate goal is an integration of people and structural planning to help the organization reach corporate goals. For example:

To develop sound, responsible organization, in tune with basic long- and short-term operating objectives of the company, able to function in terms of profit centers while not losing sight of our responsibility for achieving corporate objectives. (Small manufacturer)

To develop an organization that most effectively carries out the objectives of the company while providing an opportunity for individual employees to pursue their individual goals. (Philip Morris, Incorporated)

To insure, as nearly as possible, that organization is attuned to changing conditions and that adequate manpower is being developed for all management positions as they become vacant. (Insurance company)

The final variation of the organization-development goal focuses on building an effective organization structure, staffed by effective people, with a view toward achieving corporate objectives in a challenging and changing world. Some representative statements were as follows:

## Purposes and Objectives of the Function

To recommend modifications, in organization and people, essential to the maintenance of continuing corporate effectiveness in a dynamic, rapidly growing industry. (Major airline)

To provide for continuity of sound organization and management, and improve our competitive position. (Large retailer)

To keep available the most effective organization and people to develop and handle business under changing conditions. (Transportation company)

To advise on the types of organization and people required for the future operations of a larger and more diversified company. (Chemical company)

### Statements of Functional Activities

Some presidents simply stated that the goal of organization is to handle organization matters. The goal in these companies was variously reported as:

To teach recognition that organization development is a continual rather than intermittent function, and that an organization department provides a means of assuring that organization changes are made. (Large oil company)

To provide operating management with sound counsel and assistance on organization-development matters. (Large manufacturer)

To provide a more definitive representation of this increasingly vital function. (Large bank)

To provide staff guidance over evolving organization changes. (Large utility)

### Summary of Presidents' Goals

The goals reported by presidents range from "no separate goals" to specific goals, of which three predominated in the goal statements: (1) "to build an effective organization structure" (organization planning; (2) "to build effective management teams"; and (3) "to integrate goals 1 and 2" (organization development).

Each of these goals has several variations. It is interesting to note the relative frequency with which each was mentioned by the presidents.

Of 167 presidents responding, approximately 26 percent (43) listed organization-development goals: "to build effective organization, management, and employee teams." Seventeen percent (28) of the presidents provided organization-planning goals such as "to build an effective organization structure." Thirteen percent (22) reported the goal as "to build an effective management team." Twelve percent (20) seemed to equate organization planning and development with personnel administration. This happened most frequently in firms that have joint personnel and organization-planning departments and that are of medium size.

Approximately 11 percent (18) of the presidents indicated that their departments are a means of achieving corporate goals. Ten percent (17) stated a goal that linked organization with the corporate-planning process. Two presidents listed goals the same as corporate goals, but neither president has an organization department. The other 17 presidents simply stated that the department is needed in order to achieve obvious goals.

These goal statements reinforce the classification of departmental activities into organization planning, organization development, and joint departments of organization with either personnel or corporate planning.

## Goals Perceived by Organization Executives

It is possible that the goals perceived by the presidents were the actual goals of their organization departments or functions at the time they were created, or even at the time of the interviews—if the presidents were close to their departments. However, it is also possible that the reported goals reflected only what the presidents believed the departments or executives were doing or should be doing. In an effort to further clarify the role of the function, organization executives also were asked to specify the primary objectives of organization planning and development.

### Personnel Goals

As anticipated, few of the executives identified organization goals with those of the company. However, a number linked them with personnel. Some who did so are members of joint personnel and organization departments. Examples of these goals follow:

*Purposes and Objectives of the Function* 63

To provide qualified incumbents and replacements for each salaried position in the system. (Texas City Refining)

To identify employees of high potential; recommend development programs for them; recruit high-potential college graduates, and follow up on their training; and audit and update compensation and benefit programs. (Conglomerate)

To effect the motivation of personnel, and select motivated people. To improve competence, and stimulate creativity and leadership. (Large manufacturer)

To minimize the number of employees and number of functions. To make maximum use of informal organization. To remain adaptive. (Major airline)

To create total implementation of results-oriented position guides and standards of performance. To make the manpower inventory audit reflect managerial skills and development needs. To create an employee reserve of capable, qualified candidates. (Comet Rice Mills)

These organization executives focused their goals on personnel activities such as recruiting, selection, staffing, and placement compensation but did not indicate how the goals were tied in with the organization. Other executives set goals identical with those of management development or executive manpower planning. For example:

To provide trained and able executives for growth and replacement in losses caused by attrition. (Copper Range)

To identify and train (or locate) future managers, and strengthen and develop existing managers. (Kelsey Hayes)

To develop plans for identifying, appraising, and developing high-potential management talent. Develop plans for managerial succession and relate them to corporate plans for expansion or contraction. (Cessna Aircraft)

To find the most effective utilization of management manpower to profit objectives and long-term growth. (Sperry Rand)

To achieve maximum utilization of available managerial talent. To obtain maximum cross-fertilization of applicable product technologies and management techniques. (Electronics manufacturer)

To identify and develop future top managers. To provide for growth of all managers and for management continuity. (St. Regis Paper)

*Structural Goals*

Another group of executives mentioned goals that emphasized the creation of an effective and efficient organization structure. At the research workshop James H. Davis, manager of organization and compensation at Alcoa, said:

Our department was created in 1962, principally to provide a more systematic way to cut overhead. Its job was to develop a cost-cutting technique (and it was so identified publicly) that would enable us to do what we do in a more equitable, more impartial, and more systematic way. Our major goal at present is a basic appraisal of our company's organization with the idea of determining whether we can reorganize into profit centers instead of having functional organizations.

Emphasis on structuring organization (the organization-planning approach) is relatively prevalent. Some executives defined the goals of their departments as the performance of specific structural activities. For example:

To assist management in the identification, definition, and grouping of functions necessary to meet its objectives. (Olympia Brewing)

To create and maintain an arrangement of authorities and responsibilities. (Major airline)

To provide organization structure, delineation of responsibilities and authority, and control necessary to the attainment of corporate plans and objectives. (Brunswick)

To continue improvement in companywide organization, manpower utilization, and definition of responsibilities, authorities, and relationships for key positions. (Standard Oil Company of California)

Other executives with this orientation stated that their goal is the improvement of the organization structure to meet corporate goals. Some examples are as follows:

To create thorough organization and formal policies to give our corporate structure and operations evenness and effectiveness. (National Homes)

To maintain a workable organization structure as a vehicle through which we can achieve a high degree of corporate success (satisfied customers, employees, and investors). (Federal Mogul Corporation)

To provide independent counsel to top management in reviewing and approving organizational change; to improve effectiveness of organization through proper structuring and elimination of organizational conflict. (Eastern Airlines)

To continually refine and improve the structure of the bank so as to provide management with a flexible and responsive vehicle which can be used to accomplish short- and long-range objectives. (Bank of America)

## Purposes and Objectives of the Function

Other executives stated that the goals of their departments were to plan and develop an effective organization structure for the present and future achievement of corporate objectives or plans. For example:

To plan and develop the organization structure best suited to the company's present and future objectives. (Food processor)

To plan for the most effective current structure, based upon company objectives and provision of flexibility for future expansion and diversification. (Large bank)

To develop an organization structure that meets current operating requirements and will be able to accommodate future expansion. (Electrical products manufacturer)

To develop a five-year organization and complement plan. To advise and counsel regarding major organization changes in two divisions. (Large bank)

To develop an efficient operating organizational structure with a flexible, hard-hitting, tough-minded capability, motivated to optimum individual and collective performance. (Samsonite Corporation)

### Structural and Human Development Goals

One group of organization executives stated that their goals are to analyze and improve the organization structure and the people in it, with a view toward increased satisfaction of corporate employees and more significant achievement of corporate goals. Since this approach probably is not as familiar to the reader as the structural approach previously described, it will be delineated in greater detail.

The philosophy and goals of this approach to organization development were stated by Donald W. Davis, president of The Stanley Works, as follows:

Organization in business institutions is dynamic and continually changes in response to events, needs, pressures, and future objectives. Change takes place in business organization as a result of these factors and occurs whether planned or unplanned. Realism demands we recognize that change of both types is bound to occur. While we continually strive to anticipate it and plan accordingly, no organization can anticipate or plan for all change. The key factor is to be able to recognize it in its early stages, to appreciate the implications, and to plan to meet them. The Stanley Works organization must be flexible, in terms of attitude and capability, so that we will be equipped to handle the change which will inevitably occur. We must be sensitive to the total environment; we must view events in perspective; we must be willing to modify the historic ways of doing things; and we must have sufficient management personnel who can effectively meet new challenges.

People are a company's most important asset. Maximum development of their talents and abilities and maximum utilization of these resources are ultimately the most important factors in the success of any organization. It is a curious phenomenon that, while a company can establish an environment which encourages men and can offer specific opportunities for development, it cannot develop men. Men develop themselves; only they can supply the ambition, the interest, the drive, and the will to accomplish.

The organization-development function must know the company thoroughly—its people, its structure, its objectives, and its plans—and suggest ways of maximizing its human resources. Actions taken to achieve this must be based on the idea of close identification of individual and company interest. There is no room for manipulation of people in The Stanley Works approach to maximizing its human resources. Based on this concept of human values, organization plans must be developed in response to the recognized needs of the company. How well the needs are appreciated and met ultimately determines the success of the enterprise. It is the function of organization development to contribute to successful performance of this management responsibility.

In the broad sense, organization development must view its contribution to the enterprise from the standpoint of the "president's office." Insofar as it can identify problems and determine solutions, which the president would do if he had the time, organization development would make its greatest contribution. Looked at in this light, every organization problem of concern to the "president's office" would be the concern of organization development. Obviously, this broadens the scope of the function and greatly enhances its opportunity to contribute more effectively to the success of the company.

The goals of the department at Kaiser were spelled out in a memorandum by Carlos Efferson, the department head. He included these long-range goals:

1. Continually study to recommend improvement in organization structure and relationships, for the purpose of making the best possible contribution to the general corporate objectives, namely: a stronger company, a more efficient company, growth in the aluminum market and in our share of the market, growth in opportunities for personal achievement, and growth in profits.
2. Continually insure that the formal organization structure is
    a. Workable and efficient: See that it fits the realities of the natural divisions of work to be done and the people to do the work;

*Purposes and Objectives of the Function* 67

  *b.* As simple as possible: See that each part can always be explained in simple and easily understood terms;
  *c.* Flexible: See that it is capable of change to meet different emphasis and different personnel.

3. See that our company combines the advantages of good formal organization practice with the advantages of our informal relationships.

  Robert Melcher, former director of the organization department at North American Rockwell, said that his department had these objectives:

To provide counsel, guidance, and viability which will enable management companywide to develop sound and viable plans of organization so as to efficiently control and direct its organizations; to effectively meet growth and expansion opportunities; and to fully utilize its human resources.

To aid and encourage management to develop and clarify its organizational missions; to delineate and effectively group the work to be performed; and to establish responsibility relationships that will enable each organization and its people to realize their mutual objectives.

  William Wrightnour, vice-president of personnel at UniRoyal, emphasized that goals of organization at his company include thinking-through better ways to control, motivate, and organize people, ideas, and structure for the attainment of corporate goals.

  Donald Taffi, vice-president of organization for Electro-Optical Systems when this study was conducted, said that his department's goals were to build an effective organization and management team to fulfill corporate objectives. He explained:

Organization development is a management function that is part of the resource management task, focusing on the human resources of the company. The top manager has responsibility for this but has delegated aspects of that responsibility to an organizational element, reporting to him, that is essentially functional in nature and looks at the people or person or function responsible for the various aspects of the available resources.

  After pointing out that organization contributes functionally to the goal achievement of the firm, Mr. Taffi emphasized that companies cannot effectively separate structural activities from personnel activities, especially in executive development.

Harvey Sherman, head of this function at The Port of New York Authority, commented that practitioners of organization planning who merely rearrange boxes on organization charts have tunnel vision. He said:

> The trouble is that too many people think organizing involves only boxes on a chart, but it is much more than that. Organizing has to directly take into account both formal and informal interrelationships, and it probably is the only function that does. So you get into all kinds of human problems—how people work together in an organization, and the like—which is more than structure. But organizing does not include the usual functions of personnel administration—industrial relations, recruitment, selection, pay plans, retirement plans, and fringe benefits. These activities don't fall within the organization-development or organization-planning function.
>
> It seems to me that whether you call the function organization development or organization planning, you're underselling it if you think of it solely in terms of the mechanics of moving boxes around. The goal of organization development or organization planning is to make the organization work effectively. To do this requires more than moving boxes. No matter how you apportion responsibilities among boxes, you (as the organization planner) have the additional responsibility of getting each unit represented by a box to work together as a team, and getting each unit to see the objectives of the total organization, not only its own objectives. There are many ways in which you can do this, such as through mobility and training. But the principal goal is to get people to work together effectively. Part of the solution may require shifting functions, but part of it is much more subtle and requires understanding of human behavior and motivation.

Although Mr. Sherman emphasized that he prefers the term "organizing" to "organization planning" or "organization development," his statements indicate concern for integration of structure and people; therefore, they are compatible with the organization-development approach described in this report.

Some other department heads emphasized the integration of structural and human activities to achieve corporate goals. These executives expressed their viewpoints as follows:

> To provide the corporation with a structure, and the qualified people to man it, to carry on the work required by plans and objectives. (W. R. Grace and Company)

> To relate organization structure and management manpower needs to company goals; to take action to obtain these objectives; and to improve managerial performance in pursuit of profit. (Crompton and Knowles)

*Purposes and Objectives of the Function* 69

To develop and maintain a team of professional managers and an organization structure which will enable the company to maximize the return on the resources available. (Consolidated Papers)

To provide the company with an effective and efficient plan to enable the attainment of their goals, and to provide a framework for personnel development. (Hormel)

Other department heads referred to effectiveness and efficiency in their stated goals:

To improve organization efficiency and develop managers for future responsibilities. (Airline)

To develop a smoothly working organization free from bottlenecks—one conducive to development of future executive leadership. (Retailer)

To develop and implement a more effective working organization. To insure a supply of competent personnel for future staffing needs. (Large utility)

To maintain an efficient organization with high morale, and to develop managers for the future. (Panhandle Eastern Pipe Line)

A number of executives reported that they integrate structural and human activities, but their goals emphasize the staffing and development of people:

To identify organization structure on a long-range basis of management talent. Development and recruitment of management talent as required to meet future manpower needs. (Pharmaceutical company)

To attain the best and most effective organization to attract, retain, and develop sufficient qualified management talent to meet our future objectives and needs. (General Time)

To provide the optimum organization, effectively staffed. (Weyerhaeuser)

To organize to meet the business objectives of the company and provide opportunity for the growth and advancement of key people. (Sun Chemical)

To coordinate organization planning and control activities for the corporation. To continuously evaluate executive and specified manpower resources and planned development of personnel. To systematically select qualified candidates, from within the corporation, for more responsible positions. (Large conglomerate)

A major emphasis in some goals is on the adaptiveness of the organization and its people to change, as shown in the following statements:

To build an effective and dynamic organization, capable of making change rapidly and providing service to our agents and policyholders effectively and efficiently. (Massachusetts Mutual Life)

To develop plans for the orderly organizational growth of the company, in a changing environment, which will enable managers and other personnel to effectively realize their potential in achieving corporate objectives. (Major airline)

To help the company adapt to internal changes so that it is organized to accomplish its objectives effectively in the future. (Oil company)

Finally, in this group there were several executives who chose as their goal the building of a better organizational climate or environment:

To help the company adopt the most usable approaches to provide a positive work climate leading to maximum commitment of management people achieving company goals. (Medium-size manufacturer)

To develop an environment where the decision makers and achievers will flourish. (Large chemical company)

### Miscellaneous Goals

As with the presidents' statements, a few goals did not fit any of these patterns. Some department heads simply listed activities such as the following:

To assist corporate and divisional management in the development and implementation of organization-development policy. (Philip Morris)

To give maximum staff assistance to the organization; to perform studies for top management, to make recommendations, and to insure continuity of my own organization. (Remington Arms)

To provide specialized assistance to management in its timing efforts to improve company profitability and promote growth. (Ford Motor Company)

To provide staff planning and control. (Minnesota Mutual Life Insurance Company)

Only two department heads represented organization as a means of achieving corporate goals:

To develop an organization that will accomplish the long-range profit and growth plans of the company. (Alan Wood Steel Company)

## Purposes and Objectives of the Function

To provide services, plans, and staff assistance to aid in the achievement of the corporate goal (increase in earnings per share). (Boise Cascade)

And two executives expressed goals similar to those of many presidents who tied organization to corporate planning or business policy planning:

To determine corporate growth objectives and develop a means to achieve them. (Anchor Hocking)

To develop an ideal organization target for the business; to set up a plan of action to accomplish this goal. (A.O. Smith)

### Summary of Organization Executives' Goals

The goals reported by organization executives ranged from statements of job responsibilities to departmental goals, and they were either the same as those listed by presidents or similar to them. They are found in three groups: (1) creating and maintaining an effective organization structure (organization planning); (2) building an effective management team by the use of management-development techniques; (3) integrating goals 1 and 2 (organization development).

Of the 112 department heads responding, 9 percent (10) listed goals the same as, or similar to, those of personnel departments; 11 percent (12) reported goals similar to those of management development departments. Many of these executives worked in joint personnel and organization planning and development departments.

Forty-three percent (48) of the department heads had organization-planning goals; 24 percent (27) had organization-development goals; and the remaining 13 percent (15) listed miscellaneous goals such as activities or corporate goals.

### Comparison of Goal Statements

Only a general comparison can be made of organization planning and development goals perceived by the presidents and the department heads, since some presidents responded when their departments did not; some presidents who responded have no department; and some department heads responded when their presidents did not. In only 91 of the participating companies did both the president and the department head respond.

The greatest difference between the two groups is that the presidents listed corporate and miscellaneous goals more than twice as often as the department heads. (See Table 5.)

TABLE 5. *Organization goal statements of company presidents and organization executives.*

| Types of goals | Presidents Number | Presidents Percent | Organization Executives Number | Organization Executives Percent |
|---|---|---|---|---|
| Integration of structural and human goals (organization development) | 43 | 26 | 27 | 24 |
| Corporate and miscellaneous goals | 37 | 22 | 15 | 13 |
| Structural goals (organization planning) | 28 | 17 | 48 | 43 |
| Human goals (management development) | 22 | 13 | 12 | 11 |
| Personnel goals | 20 | 12 | 10 | 9 |
| Unspecified goals | 17 | 10 | — | — |
| Total | 167 | 100 | 112 | 100 |

Obviously, many presidents believe that all departments should contribute to the achievement of company goals, while most department heads are primarily concerned with departmental goals. With the exception of heads of joint organization and corporate-planning departments, relatively few of them emphasized the potential tie-in between organization planning and corporate planning. Most related to current organization needs or to adapting the organization to a challenging and changing future. They did not link their function with corporate planning, financial planning, marketing strategy, or activities relating to mergers and acquisitions. It appears that organization departments may be overlooking some significant relationships.

The heads of these departments, and of other staff departments as well, may be failing to observe another important factor: They should be able to justify their existence and to express their accomplishments in terms meaningful to top managers, since these men usually determine the fate of staff functions. It is to be hoped that organization department heads will not fall into the trap that years ago ensnared some personnel administrators—that of defining goals in terms of happiness; there was (and is) no proof of a direct relationship between happiness and productivity.

The number of organization-development goals stated by company presidents and the number reported by department heads are proportionally similar. About one-fourth of the respondents seemed to have as their goals the kinds of results that come from integration of people activities and structural activities. Also, the proportion of personnel goals and management development goals varied little for the two groups. They seemed to consider management development as synonymous with organization, or to regard it as sufficiently important to be included in their goals.

The widest divergence between the two groups relates to structural goals. Almost half (43) percent of the department heads referred to structure, but only 17 percent of the presidents were thus oriented. This divergence could help explain the complaints of many organization directors that the function is not valued highly enough in their company and that they and their top management are not on the same wave length regarding goals. It also seems to verify that presidents want more than merely structural analyses—but that they are being provided with little else in a number of companies.

Many departments have indeed become enamored of symmetry and efficiency rather than other matters. Yet a majority of line executives believe that structure is just a means to an end. They are more concerned with people than with structural problems and seem to believe that they can achieve their goals with any structure if they have the right people. Therefore, the organization department that is planning-oriented is likely to have difficulty in influencing both top and middle management.

### References

1. A. Etzioni, *A Comparative Analysis of Complex Organizations* (Glencoe, Ill.: Free Press, 1961).

2. Herbert Simon, "On the Concept of Organizational Goals," *Administrative Science Quarterly* (June 1964), pp. 1–22.

3. For a challenging discussion of the goal-formation process in modern organizations, see Richard Cyert and James March, *A Behavioral Theory of the Firm* (Englewood Cliffs, N.J.: Prentice-Hall, 1965).

# 4. General Activities and Organization Planning

ONE of the main purposes in conducting this study was to clarify the range of activities performed by organization departments. The variety of activities was noted more than ten years ago by Carlos Efferson, vice-president of organization planning at Kaiser:

> As a national pattern, organization planning seems literally to be whatever you call it, and an organization-planning man is whoever the firm chooses for the job; his previous experience is, typically, unrelated to organization planning. Finally, organization planning seems to consist of whatever these people decide to do.[1]

In an earlier study the author surveyed 75 firms and found that they were performing 22 organization-department activities.[2] When the current study was begun, he sought the opinions of organization specialists and department heads and reduced the number to 18.

### ACTIVITIES REPORTED BY COMPANY PRESIDENTS AND EXECUTIVES

The 169 participating presidents were asked to indicate the functions of executives whom they consult before making decisions about various organization matters. Of 11 activities listed, determining manpower needs was mentioned with the greatest frequency: The presidents reported that they consult 124 organization executives and 125 line or operating executives before making this type of decision. This suggests that the activity is performed by the staff executive, or his department, in cooperation with the line executives responsible for the manpower under consideration.

Decision making regarding formulating or changing corporate structure also seems to be a cooperative activity, since 102 organization executives and 101 line executives are consulted by the presidents on this point. Line executives in greater numbers than organization executives were consulted about the following activities: promoting and relocating key executives (122 and 97); defining and assigning key roles and functions (112 and 97); modifying or changing corporate structure (111 and 101).

TABLE 6. *Executives whom the president consults before making decisions about 11 organization activities.* ($N = 166$)

| Activities | Organization | Personnel | Line | Other |
|---|---|---|---|---|
| Determining manpower needs | 124 | 89 | 125 | 50 |
| Formulating or changing corporate structure | 102 | 79 | 101 | 72 |
| Modifying or changing corporate structure | 101 | 89 | 111 | 68 |
| Establishing policies and directives for organization development | 100 | 90 | 84 | 67 |
| Defining and assigning key roles and functions | 97 | 86 | 112 | 64 |
| Promoting and relocating key executives | 97 | 75 | 122 | 68 |
| Selecting approaches to improving organization effectiveness | 96 | 89 | 103 | 64 |
| Determining compensation and incentives for key executives | 94 | 74 | 79 | 81 |
| Resolving key interpersonal and intergroup boundary disputes | 92 | 71 | 106 | 73 |
| Developing corporate objectives and organization plans | 83 | 81 | 108 | 95 |
| Evaluating possible mergers and acquisitions organizationally | 61 | 64 | 88 | 108 |

In making decisions about modifying or changing corporate structure, the presidents reported that they also consult 89 personnel executives—the same number that they consult about manpower needs and improving organizational effectiveness. In establishing policies and directives for organization development, the presidents reported conferring with 90 personnel executives and 100 organization executives. In developing corporate objectives and organization plans, the presidents consult 108 line executives, 95 other executives, and almost equal numbers of organization and personnel executives (83 and 81). Similarly, resolving major disputes involves 106 line executives, 92 organization specialists, and almost equal numbers of personnel and other executives (71 and 73). The largest number of other executives are consulted by presidents about mergers and acquisitions. (See Table 6.)

Participating organization executives rated the importance of the 18 activities performed by them or their departments. (See Table 7.) The number of companies in the three size groups whose executives reported performing the 18 activities are shown in Table 8.

*Frequency of Activities*

Six activities were reported most frequently by executives of larger companies, less frequently by medium-size firms, and even less often by smaller firms: (1) evaluating and making recommendations for proposed organization changes; (2) conducting organization studies and recommending changes to improve the existing organization; (3) assisting management in the identification, definition, and grouping of functions necessary to meet objectives; (4) helping management clarify role and responsibility relationships of individuals and groups; (5) advising management about organization department objectives, plans, and policies; (6) providing advice for the implementation of organization changes approved by management.

One activity was reported moderately often by all firms: establishing guidelines for analyzing, evaluating, and developing sound and effective organization.

*(Text continues on page 81)*

TABLE 7. *Importance of 18 activities performed by organization executives and departments in participating companies.*

| Activity | Very important | Important | Necessary but routine | Unimportant | No. of companies |
|---|---|---|---|---|---|
| Evaluating and making recommendations for proposed organization changes. | 52 | 29 | 3 | 0 | 84 |
| Conducting organization studies and recommending changes to improve the existing organization. | 45 | 33 | 4 | 2 | 84 |
| Assisting management in the identification, definition, and grouping of functions necessary to meet its objectives. | 42 | 39 | 6 | 1 | 88 |
| Establishing guidelines for analyzing, evaluating, and developing sound and effective organization. | 42 | 26 | 9 | 1 | 78 |
| Developing plans for identifying, appraising, and developing high-potential management talent. | 42 | 18 | 5 | 2 | 67 |
| Developing plans for managerial succession and relating them to corporate plans for expansion or contraction. | 41 | 16 | 4 | 2 | 63 |

## General Activities and Organization Planning

TABLE 7. *(continued)*

| Activity | Very important | Important | Necessary but routine | Unimportant | No. of companies |
|---|---|---|---|---|---|
| Recommending organization department objectives and policies to top management. | 40 | 41 | 3 | 2 | 86 |
| Helping management to clarify the role and responsibility relationships of individuals and groups. | 37 | 44 | 7 | 2 | 90 |
| Developing managerial compensation and incentive programs. | 34 | 22 | 2 | 1 | 59 |
| Recommending methods and programs to strengthen leadership and to improve managerial skills in problem solving and group goal setting. | 33 | 28 | 5 | 0 | 66 |
| Recommending approaches that will increase the organization's ability to adapt to change. | 32 | 40 | 6 | 3 | 81 |
| Advising management about organization department objectives, plans, and policies. | 27 | 43 | 11 | 2 | 83 |
| Providing advice about the implementation of organization changes approved by management. | 22 | 45 | 16 | 2 | 85 |

TABLE 7. *(continued)*

|  | *Importance of the Activity* |  |  |  |  |
|---|---|---|---|---|---|
| Activity | Very important | Important | Necessary but routine | Unimportant | No. of companies |
| Recommending methods and programs to improve interpersonal and intergroup relations and the company's work climate. | 21 | 32 | 7 | 3 | 63 |
| Developing programs to improve line management's effectiveness in performing organization work. | 19 | 31 | 8 | 5 | 63 |
| Providing assistance in the preparation of organization charts and position descriptions. | 15 | 25 | 38 | 6 | 84 |
| Auditing structures, procedures, supervisory ratios, and management levels, for compliance with company policy. | 14 | 32 | 15 | 7 | 68 |
| Preparing, distributing, and maintaining a manual of organization charts and position descriptions. | 14 | 26 | 43 | 2 | 85 |

*General Activities and Organization Planning*

TABLE 8. *Number of participating companies performing 18 organization activities.*

| Activity | No. of Companies Performing Activity ||| Total |
|---|---|---|---|---|
| | Large | Medium-size | Small | |
| 1 | 56 | 16 | 12 | 84 |
| 2 | 55 | 16 | 13 | 84 |
| 3 | 58 | 18 | 12 | 88 |
| 4 | 48 | 16 | 14 | 78 |
| 5 | 36 | 16 | 15 | 67 |
| 6 | 35 | 15 | 13 | 63 |
| 7 | 52 | 19 | 15 | 86 |
| 8 | 56 | 20 | 14 | 90 |
| 9 | 33 | 14 | 12 | 59 |
| 10 | 34 | 17 | 15 | 66 |
| 11 | 50 | 18 | 13 | 81 |
| 12 | 53 | 17 | 13 | 83 |
| 13 | 53 | 19 | 13 | 85 |
| 14 | 36 | 16 | 11 | 63 |
| 15 | 39 | 15 | 9 | 63 |
| 16 | 52 | 17 | 15 | 84 |
| 17 | 43 | 14 | 11 | 68 |
| 18 | 52 | 16 | 17 | 85 |

Note: See Table 7 for an explanation of the activities in column 1.

Five activities were reported least frequently by larger firms, more frequently by medium-size companies, and even more often by smaller firms: (1) developing plans for identifying, appraising, and developing high-potential management talent; (2) recommending methods and programs to strengthen leadership and improve managerial skills in problem solving and group goal setting; (3) recommending organization objectives to top management; (4) providing assistance in the preparation of organization charts and position descriptions; (5) preparing, distributing, and maintaining a manual of organization charts and position descriptions.

Four activities were reported as infrequently performed by companies of all sizes: (1) recommending methods and programs to improve interpersonal and intergroup relations and the company's work climate; (2) developing programs to improve line management's effectiveness in performing organizational work; (3) developing plans for managerial succession and relating them to corporate plans for expansion or contraction; (4) developing managerial compensation and incentive programs.

*Importance of Activities*

The activities they performed were rated in importance by the participating executives. In analyzing their ratings, the following values were assigned to each classification: *Very important,* 4; *important,* 3; *necessary but routine,* 2; *unimportant,* 1.

To account for variance in the number of companies performing each activity, the raw scores were converted to an index by the following method: The number of ratings were multiplied by the value of each rating, and this amount was divided by the frequency of response for each activity. Using this index of importance, the activities were ranked 1 through 18 (most important to least important) for companies in the three size groups. (See Table 9.)

Three activities were rated highly important by companies of all sizes: (1) recommending methods and programs to improve interpersonal and intergroup relations and the company's work climate; (2) developing plans for managerial succession and relating them to corporate plans for expansion or contraction; (3) developing managerial compensation and incentive programs.

Three activities were rated moderately important by companies of all sizes: (1) establishing guidelines for analyzing, evaluating, and developing sound and effective organization; (2) evaluating and making recommendations for proposed organization changes; (3) conducting organization studies and recommending changes to improve the existing organization.

Three activities were rated least important by companies of all sizes: (1) preparing, distributing, and maintaining a manual of organization charts and position descriptions; (2) providing assistance in the preparation of organization charts and position descriptions; (3) providing advice about the implementation of organization changes approved by management.

Three activities were rated more important by larger companies

TABLE 9. *Importance of organization activities in participating companies (ranked 1–18 by index of importance).*

|  | Ranking in Importance | | | |
| --- | --- | --- | --- | --- |
| Activity | Large companies (N = 61) | Medium-size companies (N = 33) | Small companies (N = 18) | All companies (N = 112) |
| 1 | 12 | 5 | 6 | 9 |
| 2 | 10 | 6 | 10 | 9 |
| 3 | 14 | 13 | 5 | 11 |
| 4 | 7 | 7 | 7 | 7 |
| 5 | 4 | 4 | 11 | 3 |
| 6 | 3 | 3 | 4 | 2 |
| 7 | 11 | 15 | 13 | 10 |
| 8 | 15 | 10 | 9 | 13 |
| 9 | 1 | 2 | 2 | 1 |
| 10 | 2 | 12 | 15 | 4 |
| 11 | 8 | 16 | 12 | 14 |
| 12 | 17 | 11 | 8 | 12 |
| 13 | 16 | 18 | 14 | 18 |
| 14 | 6 | 1 | 3 | 5 |
| 15 | 5 | 8 | 1 | 6 |
| 16 | 13 | 17 | 16 | 15 |
| 17 | 9 | 9 | 18 | 16 |
| 18 | 18 | 14 | 17 | 17 |

Note: See Table 7 for an explanation of the activities in column 1.

but declined in importance among medium-size firms and were considered even less important by smaller firms: (1) auditing structures, procedures, supervisory ratios, and management levels for compliance to company policy; (2) recommending methods and programs to strengthen leadership and improve managerial skills in problem solving and group goal setting; (3) developing plans for identifying, appraising, and developing high-potential management talent.

The ratings for three activities were in a reverse pattern. These activities were considered unimportant by the larger companies; but the smaller the firm, the more important the activity became: (1) assisting management in the identification, definition, and grouping functions necessary to meet its objectives; (2) helping management clarify the role and responsibility relationships of individuals and groups; (3) advising management about organization department objectives, plans, and policies.

And three activities were rated about the same by large and smaller companies, but differently by medium-size firms. Rated very important by large and smaller companies, but only moderately important by medium-size firms, was this activity: developing programs to improve line management's effectiveness in performing organization work.

Rated moderately important by large and smaller companies, but unimportant by medium-size firms, was the following activity: recommending approaches that would increase the organization's ability to adapt to change.

Also rated moderately important by large and smaller companies, but slightly more important by medium-size firms, was this activity: recommending organization department objectives and policies to top management.

Several differences in the data about the importance and frequency of organization activities reflect the differences that exist between the two basic approaches to organization—planning and development.

## Operating Patterns of Organization Planning

Organization planning, which emphasizes structural activities, is the approach that apparently arrived first on the corporate scene. In organization planning, organization problems are solved by adjusting the organization itself. Proposed changes usually refer to reporting relationships and organization charts rather than to the people in the organization.

Organization development, the second approach, emphasizes relationships and the people who hold positions in the structure. Proposed changes in structure and staff include attempts to change attitudes and relationships between people by the use of group dynamics and similar techniques.

Many of the differences in company approaches to organization exist because of company policies, the history of the department, its

*General Activities and Organization Planning* 85

age, and the beliefs of corporate management, as well as those of the company's staff and operating executives.

Case histories of several companies that emphasize organization-structure analysis are presented here with their statements of objectives and the activities performed by their organization departments. These companies—which include a container company, an airline, a metal-products manufacturer, an aircraft manufacturer, and an oil company—seem to be representative of the more traditional approach to organization.

*Large Container Company*

The development of the function in a major container company is interesting because it includes both approaches to organization. The company's director of organization planning provided the following historical background:

There has been an organization-planning unit within the company for a number of years; however, in 1966 the position of vice-president of organization planning was created, reporting to the chairman of the board and responsible essentially for the development of policies, plans, and programs, and their audit as they relate to the activities of organization, personnel, and compensation. The administration of these functions remained in the employee relations department.

This move was taken to give emphasis to the needed consideration and development of our employees as human resources, as well as to provide more adequately for planning. . . . The arrangement served to initiate a number of significant programs which have already begun to contribute to the planning and development of our human-resource needs.

(The position description of the vice-president of organization planning in this company appears in Exhibit 1.)

During the summer of 1966, the vice-president of organization planning was put in charge of the employee relations department in addition to his own department. However, the functions of organization planning and organization administration continued to operate within the employee relations department, as before.

(The position descriptions of the director of organization planning and the manager of organization administration are shown in Exhibits 2 and 3.)

**Exhibit 1.** *Position description of vice-president of organization planning (large container company).*

*Objective:* To develop, recommend, and audit the administration of policies, plans, and programs to provide the managers, the professional and technical people, and the organization needed to achieve our corporate objectives.

*Basic policy*

1. Our policy is to encourage individual growth through the achievement of personal goals which in turn support the company's objectives, and also to recognize and reward the attainment of those goals.
2. We believe personal growth is greatest when the individual is challenged by the requirements of his position and when his potential matches these requirements.
3. We also believe an organization structure clearly defined in terms of objectives, policy, functions, and working relationships furthers the growth of our people by making it easier for them to attain their personal objectives, which in turn support the corporate objectives.

*Major results expected*

1. To fulfill the "Universal Responsibilities of Management Positions" [company policy guide].
2. To develop, recommend, and audit the administration of organizational policies, plans, and programs for the company relating to organizational planning, management, professional and technical personnel planning, compensation planning, and personnel research.
3. To initiate, define, formalize, and audit the administration of policies, plans, and programs required to provide the organization structure involving functions, position, and working relationships for the company's entire field of operation and all management, professional, and technical positions.
4. To guide and work closely with managers in the understanding and effective use of the organizational tools and in the administration of organizational policies, procedures, and plans.
5. To keep up to date on the corporate objectives, the business plan, and company policies and trends and changes in the company's field of operation; and to plan and develop the organizational adjustments required to effectively cope with these trends and changes and achieve the corporate objectives.
6. To audit and evaluate the established organizational policies, plans, and programs in terms of their cost and effectiveness in meeting objectives, and initiate improvements where necessary.

*General Activities and Organization Planning* 87

EXHIBIT 2. *Position description of director of organization planning (large container company).*

*Objective:* To develop, recommend, and audit the administration of policies, plans, and programs required to provide the organization structure necessary to achieve our corporate objectives.

*Basic policy*

1. We recognize that organization structure is a dynamic tool and must be flexible enough to meet the needs of a growing company.
2. We will seek active participation by managers in planning the organization. The planning of each organization unit must start with a clear understanding of the objectives of that unit and the relationship of those objectives to the corporate objectives and the business plan.
3. We believe well-stated organization structures must be clearly defined in terms of objectives, policy, functions, and working relationships stemming from the corporate objectives and business plan; and further the growth of our people through allowing for the attainment of their personal objectives, which in turn support the corporate objectives.

*Major results expected*

1. To fulfill the "Universal Responsibilities of Management Positions."
2. To initiate, define, formalize, and audit administration of the policies, plans, and programs required to provide the organization structure, in terms of functions, positions, and working relationships, for the company's entire fields of operation and all management, professional, and technical positions.
3. To provide guidance and work closely with managers in the understanding and effective use of the organization tool and in the administration of organization policies, procedures, and plans.
4. To keep up to date on the corporate objectives, business plan, and policies and trends and changes in the company's field of operation; to plan and develop the adjustments in organization required to effectively cope with these trends and changes and achieve the corporate objectives.
5. To prepare audits and evaluations of the established organization in terms of its cost and effectiveness in meeting objectives, and initiate improvements where necessary.

EXHIBIT 3. *Position description of manager of organization administration (large container company).*

*Objective:* To administer and participate in the development and recommendation of policies, plans, and programs required to provide the organization structure necessary to achieve our corporate objectives and the business plan.

*Basic policy*

1. We recognize that organization structure is a dynamic tool and must be flexible enough to meet the needs of a growing company.
2. We will seek active participation by managers in planning the organization in relationship to their unit objectives with corporate and business-plan objectives. We will work closely and participate with the organization-planning department in the administration of policies and plans developed by the department.
3. We believe well-stated organization structures must be clearly defined in terms of objectives, policy, functions, and working relationships stemming from the corporate objectives and business plan; and further the growth of our people through allowing for the attainment of their personal objectives, which in turn support the corporate objectives.

*Major functions and responsibilities*

1. To fulfill the "Universal Responsibilities of Management Positions."
2. To plan, control, and coordinate the administration of policies, plans, and programs required to provide the organization structure, in terms of functions, positions, and working relationships, for the company's entire fields of operation and all management, professional, and technical positions.
3. To conduct organization studies as requested, or as deemed advisable; and to develop, with department management, the organization's objectives in relation to corporate objectives and the business plan, statements of policy and organization structures based on logical operating relationships within and between organizational components.
4. To coordinate the development of position descriptions and related documents with responsible managers for all management, professional, and technical personnel to clearly define areas of responsibility and accountability and to provide guidance in employment, placement, evaluation, and training and development activities.
5. To keep up to date on the corporate objectives, business plan, and policies and trends and changes in the company's field of operation; to plan and develop the adjustments in organization required to effectively cope with these trends and changes and achieve the corporate objectives.
6. To develop necessary control and administrative procedures relative to the implementation, administration, evaluation, and interpretation of organization-administration programs, instructions, manuals, announcements, and related documents; and initiate improvements where necessary.

---

In mid-1967, organization planning was merged with employee relations. Apparently, the company was changing its orientation from organization planning to organization development, since it was beginning to integrate activities relating to structural changes with those relating to individual growth changes. However, the director of organization planning continued to be concerned primarily with structural problems, as his position description indicates. Furthermore, although it is possible that the organization planners coordinate with appropriate persons in employee relations about organization-development problems, they are not explicitly delegated the responsibility for this activity.

## Major Airline

The organization-planning function of the airline reports to the vice-president of management services and control, and its activities include editing, publishing, and distributing companywide regulations; assuring continuous monitoring and development of company reports and forms; providing organization structure, job analysis, and job evaluation, and an organization-planning service to all company elements.

The company has developed policies and principles of organization, and some definite guidelines for the organization function. These statements, given in Exhibit 4, clearly emphasize structural analysis and change.

EXHIBIT 4. *Statements of organization policy, principles, and responsibilities (major airline).*

---

### Organization

The company's organization policy comprises three principal tenets:

A. Centralized control of system operations, equipment routing, and space management. This establishes one production line, one production planning and control center.
B. Central staff development, system service policies, methods, and procedures. The company must achieve consistency in appearance throughout the system so that it presents the same public image in all areas.
C. Decentralized administration. The size and geographical characteristics of the company make it necessary for decisions to be delegated to the lowest possible element of organization at which they will be intelligently made. This becomes increasingly important as the company grows.

The organization structure should:

A. Assure that all functions essential to meeting the organization's objectives are assigned to logical elements of the organization.
B. Utilize to the optimum the skills and abilities of available personnel.
C. Provide for short and direct lines of communication by keeping the number of organization units and levels of authority at a minimum.
D. Maintain flexibility so that the organization can be modified for changing needs without major realignment of basic functions.
E. Provide for clear lines of authority from top to bottom.

The following guides should be used when planning organization changes:

A. Related functions should be combined when practicable.
B. Responsibilities and authority must be clearly defined for complete understanding.
C. No function should be assigned to more than one independent element of the organization.
D. Each member of the organization should report to only one supervisor.
E. Assistants should not be placed in a line capacity between executive and subordinate levels.
F. Authority to act must match responsibility to accomplish.
G. A definite distinction between line, staff, and functional authority and responsibility should be understood and maintained.
H. Authority for establishing major policies should be placed at key points to provide proper direction and control.
I. Responsibility and authority for implementing policy should be decentralized and delegated to the greatest extent possible.
J. The number of subordinates reporting to one supervisor should be determined by evaluating the capabilities of individuals involved and the nature of their responsibilities.

Line, staff, and functional responsibility:

A. Line responsibility and authority permit issuance of orders, supervision of activities, and other controls over the working group. Line authority is the direct administrative control over the activity. Personnel having line authority should be strong in administrative ability, which includes planning, organizing, and controlling the performance of subordinates. Technical knowledge in the field of activity is desirable, but the primary requisite is the talent for getting work done through others.
B. Staff responsibility and authority permit obtaining information, rendering advice, and furnishing ideas. They provide for no administrative authority over individuals in the line organization. Staff personnel should be well grounded in the technical knowledge required in their particular jobs. They should also possess innovative ability and the ability to work with others on a basis of mutual understanding and cooperation. Administrative ability is not necessarily a requisite for staff jobs.

### General Activities and Organization Planning

C. Functional responsibility is an extension of staff responsibilities. It includes development of standards and policies to be recommended to line organizations; preparation of procedural and method data to implement such recommendations; furnishing of technical or otherwise specialized advice and assistance in the application of such procedures; and monitoring of activities for compliance, to bring instances of nonconformance to the attention of line organization management. Personnel in positions of functional authority should have the same basic abilities as staff personnel, plus the administrative ability to plan, organize, and control the work of their subordinates. In such positions, ability to innovate and to work with others is even more important than in staff positions. Also, judgment is a significant factor because of the influence which a functional position's recommendations has on line decisions.

The company's organization structure is based on an original plan which provided for six levels of supervision, identified as administration, department, division, section, group, and unit.

Establishment of a new organization element requires approval based on level, as shown in the accompanying chart.

| Element | Approval required | Directed by |
|---|---|---|
| Administration | Board of directors | Senior vice-president, vice-president |
| Department | President | vice-president, director, corporate officer |
| Division | Executive vice-president, senior vice-president, or head of organization reporting directly to the president | *director, manager of (function) |
| Section | Department director or above | (function) manager |
| Group | | Chief, (function) manager, general foreman |
| Unit | | Supervisor, foreman |

* Approval of the president is required for use of director title.

The decision as to which level will be recommended for an organization element will be reached in discussions between the headquarters organization concerned and the organization-planning division. Judgment will be a major factor. The following guides may be used:

A. An administration is a major element of the company, the fundamental re-

sponsibilities of which are unique in character and substantial in scope, and have a major effect on overall company activities.
B. A department is a primary function of the company, the responsibilities of which are of lesser magnitude than those of an administration. This type of organization is part of an administration. The department level is also used for functions which are broad in scope and unique in character, but carry responsibilities which are more strictly functional or staff than operational in nature.
C. A division is a primary function of the department, having the same characteristics within a department's area of responsibility as the two top organization levels have within theirs.
D. Section, group, and unit are primary elements of division, section, and group, respectively.

## The Stanley Works

The Stanley Works also follows an organization-planning approach, as indicated by the position description of its director of organization development (Exhibit 5) and the statement of services provided by the department (Exhibit 6). These documents indicate an emphasis on structural activities (position descriptions, titles, and charts) and on executive inventory and recruiting activities. There is no evidence that the department attempts to integrate organization and manpower plans with behavioral-change approaches, or environmental-change analysis, both of which are evident in companies that employ the organization-development approach.

The focus is on improvement of structure by means of analysis, charts, position descriptions, and policy manuals. Little or no attention is focused on the human-relations factors.

EXHIBIT 5. *Position description of director of organization development (The Stanley Works).*

Position title: Director of organization development     Division: Corporate

Reports to: Director of employee and public relations

*Function:* To assist in providing and developing a constantly strengthening organization for the future operation of all segments of The Stanley Works, through assuring that the organization is developed in depth for the most effective utilization of managerial and specialist capacities and that an adequate reserve of manpower will be available to supply future needs.

## General Activities and Organization Planning

*Responsibilities*

Within the limits of his approved programs and the policies and procedures of the company, the director of organization development is responsible for the fulfillment of the duties set forth here.

A. Planning

He will formulate, in conjunction with top management, long- and short-range plans for the development of the company and divisional organizations, both as they relate to organization structuring and to the management personnel within the company and divisions. These plans, when approved, will constitute the programs of the director of organization development. They will include but not be limited to programs for:
1. Defining and describing the responsibilities, authorities, and relationships of management and specialist positions.
2. Reviewing and recommending changes in organizational relationships and the distribution of responsibilities.
3. Developing and applying methods for appraising performance and measuring the potential for growth of management and specialist personnel, and hence for determining current and future organization needs of the company.
4. Developing and applying methods for recruiting and selecting potential executive and professional personnel, both within and outside the company.

B. Operations

As a staff executive whose operations influence all components of the company, with full recognition that decentralization with its corresponding delegation of responsibility and authority is one of the governing policies of the company, the director of organization development is responsible for:
1. The maintenance of charts and position descriptions covering executive, administrative, and professional positions.
2. The maintenance of an inventory of all executive, administrative, and professional personnel throughout the company as a clearinghouse for transfers, promotions, and placement of qualified personnel from within the company where they are needed or where job opportunities occur.
3. The maintenance of personnel files covering executive, administrative, and professional personnel.
4. The identification, through appraisals, of needs for development of managerial and professional personnel; and the formulation, with them and their line supervisors, of appropriate plans and programs for their training and development. Such plans may require individual action such as attendance at appropriate seminars or courses of study, job rotation, and the like; or, on occasion, group sessions for discussion and direct training.
5. Coordination of the recruitment of executive and specialist trainees from among college seniors and graduates, or equivalent sources, for future organization strengthening.

6. Periodic and continuing audits of the progress and development of actual and potential executive, administrative, and professional personnel, with recommendations for preventive or remedial action as needed.

*Relationships*

The director of organization development will establish and maintain the following relationships and be accountable for their proper observance:
A. With senior executives
   1. He will solicit the active cooperation of division managers and other senior executives in the planning and implementation of his approved programs.
   2. He will provide advice and assistance to them, with respect to the needs for development among their subordinate personnel, and related plans and programs, in accordance with the objectives of the company.
   3. He will provide a management and specialist "clearinghouse placement service" to division managers and other senior executives of the company, as requested.
B. With the industrial relations department
   1. He will communicate and coordinate with the industrial relations department on all matters of mutual concern, especially in the area of training.
   2. He will utilize the services, as needed, of the industrial relations department, and will provide such assistance as may be appropriate, as requested.
C. With division personnel departments
   1. He will communicate and coordinate with division personnel departments on all matters of mutual concern, especially in the areas of training and development, recruiting, selection and placement of college graduates, and identification of potential executive, administrative, and professional manpower.
   2. He will utilize the testing services of division personnel departments, as needed, and provide appropriate assistance on request.

---

EXHIBIT 6. *Statement of services performed by organization development for divisions and corporate management (The Stanley Works).*

---

Services performed for both the divisions and corporate management

1. Structuring organization
   Writing position descriptions and maintaining a complete file.
   Establishing and maintaining a system to insure uniformity of position titles.
   Maintaining accurate, up-to-date charts of organization throughout the corporation.
   Identifying organization-structure needs and problems (short- and long-range), and investigating and recommending solutions.
2. Staffing and developing organization
   Providing a clearinghouse for interdivisional transfers—making evaluations and recommendations.

### General Activities and Organization Planning

Conducting outside searches for key-level personnel—evaluating and recommending.
Interviewing and screening candidates—both outside and inside—for other key positions.
Promoting and guiding corporate trainee programs—M.B.A., foreman trainees, etc.
Conducting career-counseling interviews.
Conducting regular evaluation interviews involving high-potential younger men in the company.
Guiding the administration of the "Miller program."
Maintaining specific types of skill inventories.
Maintaining personnel files for all exempt employees in the company.
Identifying individual needs for training—making specific recommendations for inside or outside training activity.
Maintaining close surveillance of compensation status of appropriate groups of exempt employees; making specific recommendations concerning individuals and college-trainee rate ranges.
Conducting training courses involving principles of organization.
Providing advice and counsel to managers concerning their internal organization problems.
Conducting annual manpower-planning audits with division general managers.
Reviewing corporate and divisional long-range plans; recommending with regard to organizational implications.

3. Assessing organizational effectiveness
Promoting and assisting the goals-and-objectives programs.
Administering the annual performance-review program; analyzing and making recommendations.
Gathering and analyzing organizational data and statistics; making recommendations.

Services performed for corporate management only

1. Developing an annual management-manpower inventory and report.
2. Providing advice and counsel concerning senior management organizational problems.
3. Conducting specific studies and investigations, as required.
4. Making recommendations concerning broad corporate organization structuring problems—both overseas and domestic.

---

## Lockheed Aircraft Corporation

At Lockheed, the purpose of organization planning is to:

provide assistance, on a staff basis, to corporate and division management in their responsibility for organization planning, including advice and counsel in the development of overall organization plans; assistance to management in the definition of its functions and responsibilities; and staff service to corporate management in its development of management operating policies.

The corporate director of organization planning is delegated the responsibility for this function. His responsibilities are described in his position description, which is shown in Exhibit 7.

EXHIBIT 7. *Position description of corporate director of organization planning (Lockheed Aircraft Corporation).*

### Specific Responsibilities

Organization planning

To continually appraise the organization structure of the corporation staffs and divisions, and make appropriate recommendations to corporate and divisional management, as required.

To prepare, issue, and maintain a corporate manual of organization, including approved organization charts of the corporation and its divisions. To assist concerned divisions and staffs in the development of statements of functions and responsibilities for issuance in appropriate divisional or corporate organization manuals.

To review and evaluate for the chief executive officer, the corporate policy committee, and the president and his staff, as requested, proposals and recommendations relating to the organization structure, delegation of functions and responsibilities, and related overall corporate operating policies; and submit appropriate recommendations.

To review organization plans and programs of divisions and staffs, including organization charts, statements of functions and responsibilities, and organization-change notices, for information and for conformity to established overall corporate organization structure.

To assist corporate and division management, upon request, in the analysis and evaluation of operating problems related to organization matters; and submit appropriate recommendations, as required.

To keep continually informed of contemplated changes in company objectives and plans; and determine their effect, if any, on established organization structures and related operating policies.

Policies and procedures

To assist, along with other concerned corporate staffs, in the development of management policy statements defining corporate operating policy as established by the corporate policy committee or its delegates.

### General Activities and Organization Planning

To receive proposals from divisions and staffs for revisions or additions to corporate management policy statements; arrange for consideration of these proposals by the policy committee (or the president and his staff); assist concerned functional staffs in the development of statements reflecting approved corporate policy; and publish and maintain a corporate manual of such management policy statements.

To assist corporate and division management, upon request, in the analysis and evaluation of operating problems related to overall corporate policy matters, and submit appropriate recommendations, as required; and participate as necessary in the preparation of appropriate management policy statements.

To review for the corporate policy committee, or its delegates, proposed revisions of established corporate policy statements from the viewpoint of adherence to established and approved organization structure and alignment; and submit appropriate recommendations, as required.

General

To establish and maintain such specific operating procedures and practices, both internal and companywide, as are necessary to assure that the assigned organization-planning responsibilities are carried out.

To maintain a continuing staff relationship with divisional organization-planning groups, and provide staff counsel and service to these groups upon request.

To periodically review the administration of the divisional organization-planning staffs, and submit appropriate recommendations to divisional and corporate management, as required.

To maintain a continuing awareness of organization-planning developments and trends throughout industry, evaluate their potential application within Lockheed, and submit appropriate recommendations.

The corporate director is accountable to the vice-president of administration for carrying out the foregoing responsibilities and any others which may be assigned to him.

---

Again, the pattern is one of structural orientation, with less attention on behavioral factors.

### Standard Oil Company of California

Standard Oil Company of California created the first viable department of organization in the United States in the 1930s. Its scope of activity is shown in Exhibit 8, and its functions in Exhibit 9. The

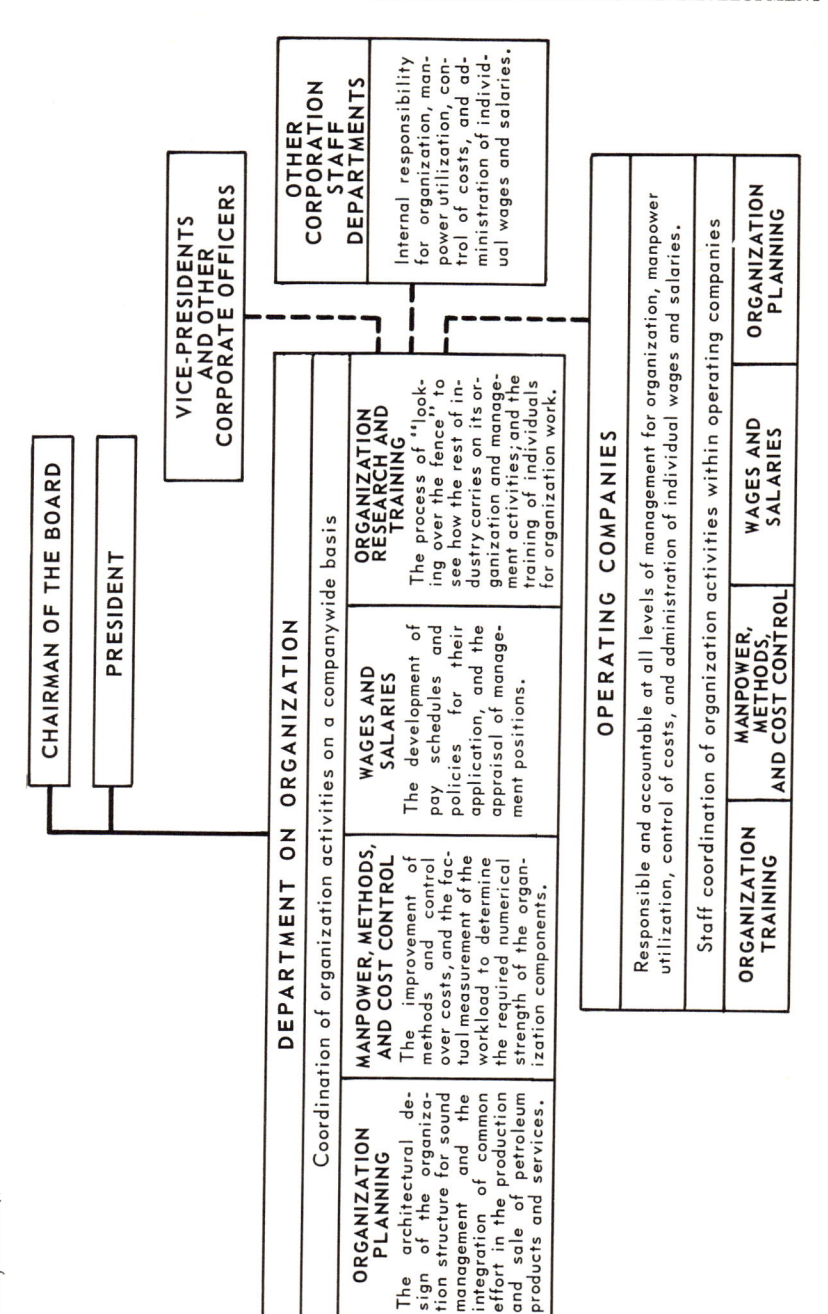

EXHIBIT 8. *Organizational relationship and responsibility, department on organization (Standard Oil Company of California).*

```
                    ┌─────────────────────┐
                    │ CHAIRMAN OF THE BOARD│
                    └──────────┬──────────┘
                               │
                    ┌──────────┴──────────┐
                    │      PRESIDENT      │
                    └──────────┬──────────┘
                               │
              ┌────────────────┼────────────────┐
              │                                 │
    ┌─────────┴──────────┐              ┌───────┴────────┐
    │ VICE-PRESIDENTS    │              │     OTHER      │
    │      AND OTHER     │- - - - - - - │  CORPORATION   │
    │ CORPORATE OFFICERS │              │     STAFF      │
    └────────────────────┘              │  DEPARTMENTS   │
                                        └────────────────┘
```

**DEPARTMENT ON ORGANIZATION**

Coordination of organization activities on a companywide basis

| ORGANIZATION PLANNING | MANPOWER, METHODS, AND COST CONTROL | WAGES AND SALARIES | ORGANIZATION RESEARCH AND TRAINING |
|---|---|---|---|
| The architectural design of the organization structure for sound management and the integration of common effort in the production and sale of petroleum products and services. | The improvement of methods and control over costs, and the factual measurement of the workload to determine the required numerical strength of the organization components. | The development of pay schedules and policies for their application, and the appraisal of management positions. | The process of "looking over the fence" to see how the rest of industry carries on its organization and management activities; and the training of individuals for organization work. |

**OTHER CORPORATION STAFF DEPARTMENTS**

Internal responsibility for organization, manpower utilization, control of costs, and administration of individual wages and salaries.

**OPERATING COMPANIES**

Responsible and accountable at all levels of management for organization, manpower utilization, control of costs, and administration of individual wages and salaries.

Staff coordination of organization activities within operating companies

| ORGANIZATION TRAINING | MANPOWER, METHODS, AND COST CONTROL | WAGES AND SALARIES | ORGANIZATION PLANNING |
|---|---|---|---|

*General Activities and Organization Planning*

EXHIBIT 9. *Statement of functional responsibility, department on organization (Standard Oil Company of California).*

## Department on Organization

Function

The department on organization develops policies and plans to guide members of management within the corporation and operating companies in the discharge of their primary responsibility for (1) organization; (2) manpower utilization; (3) control of costs; (4) administration of individual wages and salaries.

It furnishes functional advice and assistance to officers and other members of management of the corporation, operating companies, and affiliates. Periodically, it appraises the effectiveness of the efforts of these organizations in connection with the foregoing responsibilities. The principal functions of the department are listed in following paragraphs.

Organization planning

The design and development of organization structures for all segments of the corporation and operating companies, and the formulation of overall organization policies. This includes review of the objectives and structure of the corporation, operating companies, and affiliates, and presentation of recommendations thereon. The department also counsels and assists in preparing management guides.

At the direction of the chairman of the board or the president, the department also renders service to governmental agencies, charitable organizations, welfare groups, schools and universities, trade associations, and other companies and industries, by conducting surveys and preparing recommendations on organization and management matters.

Manpower, methods, and cost control

Specific reviews of operations and methods, and recommendations for improvements leading to better utilization of manpower, facilities, and money. Surveys of components of the corporation and operating companies are made, as required, to determine the effectiveness of manpower utilization, methods, and cost control.

Wages and salaries

The planning and development of sound and uniform wage and salary schedules. Functional guidance is provided to management throughout the corporation and operating companies. Periodically, an appraisal is made of wage and salary administration and job and position evaluation. Wage and salary practices are frequently compared with those of other petroleum companies, and periodically with local industries and with industry in general. Position and job description policies and procedures originate within the department and are the basis for functional guidance. The department serves as a research and fact-finding agency on wage and salary matters, and renders consulting service to the various organization components.

Organization research and training

Research and special surveys in organization to develop and disseminate the best thought and practice on organization, manpower utilization, methods, wages and salaries, and the processes of their administration. This research, together with the wide experience gained in normal activities, has led to the preparation of several books by members of the department: *Top Management Organization and Control; The Functions of Corporate Secretaries, Treasurers, and Comptrollers; The Coordination of Motive, Men, and Money in Industrial Research; The Management Guide;* and *More Profit—Less Paper*. To provide uniform application of established principles of organization, the department provides training and indoctrination for organization personnel, and coordinates such training carried on by other organizational components.

---

department conducts extensive studies and provides important guidelines for Standard Oil of California's executives. One such aid is the famous monograph, prepared by Joseph Lucas with the assistance of the department, *More Profit—Less Paper*. This is a guide on company reduction of administrative and clerical work. A major continuing activity of the department, however, is the organization and manpower survey. These studies are conducted according to the following outline:

1. *Preliminary planning*
   Origination and approval to go ahead.
   Project manager selection.
   Project work-order preparation and approval.
   Survey-team selection and scheduling.
   Advance communication.
2. *Field work*
   Determination of present organization: jobs and men.
   Interviews, observations, questionnaires, logs.
   Relationships with other organizations.
   Team meetings, development of recommendations.
3. *Close-out and preparation of final report*
   Close-out with field and home office management.
   Implementation of recommendations, modifications, follow-up.

The preliminary planning phase includes the following steps and, importantly, uses line personnel as part of the team that conducts the organization and manpower study. As the Standard Oil Company of California manual outlines it:

*Project origination*

A Department on Organization Survey usually originates through a request by a company officer to survey some unit or function for which he is responsible, or through a request by the head of some unit of the company wanting assistance on a survey. It may be a survey suggested by the department on organization as a part of the continuing program to survey all major units of the company at appropriate intervals.

*Project manager*

After preliminary discussion with the originator to receive and define the project, a project manager is selected and assigned the project, with the responsibility for carrying it to completion.

The project manager first familiarizes himself with the subject, to the extent possible, through files and correspondence, previous studies of the subject or related organizations of functions, organization charts, job descriptions, and discussions with people experienced or knowledgeable in the field. He will then prepare a project work order and present it through channels for approval.

*Project work order*

The project work order defines the project, states the objective and includes a plan of work and schedule for execution of the survey. In developing the plan of approach and the schedules, the project manager must consider such factors as the type and size of the organization to be studied; the functions to be included or omitted; the time available for the project; the depth of investigation required to get the desired answers; and then must estimate the amount of field work that will be required. Upon approval, the project work order is assigned a number. It becomes the authority for undertaking the survey, within the scope limits specified in the project work order, and in addition becomes the means for accumulating and recording expenses charged to the project.

*Team size*

The size of the survey team depends upon the size of the organization to be studied, the type of organization, the amount of field interviewing that must be done, the overall elapsed time available for the project, and the objectives. If the size of the project is such that a team of more than about five members will be required, the team will probably have to be divided into two or more subgroups, each studying assigned units or functions. In this event, the project manager must coordinate and pull together the separate survey activities into an integrated final result.

*Team selection*

Selection of candidates for the team is made by the project manager, working closely with the executive development staff and with counsel of appropriate management, and with the originator of the project. Team membership must meet the approval of the manager, department on organization, who carries final responsibility for all such surveys. Team members are selected with the objective of bringing together the best combination of appropriate backgrounds and analytical skills available. Membership will usually include men from the organization being studied, so as to be able to draw on their specific knowledge. Members may also be selected from organization units performing similar functions elsewhere in the corporation or operating companies; and some may be selected from "client" or "customer" organizations to aid in exploring relationships and interfaces between the unit under study and the other departments it deals with. One reason for selecting team members from related organizations is because they become indoctrinated with the thinking of the survey team and can assist management later in working out details during implementation of the recommendations. Sometimes local organization and cost-control staff people are selected because of their local knowledge, analytical talents, and opportunities to learn for later application of new knowledge in their regular jobs. Large survey teams may include a compensation analyst who can advise currently on wage or salary matters encountered or resulting from recommendations, in addition to serving as a regular survey team member.

*Responsibilities of team members*

Each team member is expected to be a fully participating member, relieved of all other responsibilities while on the survey, responsible to the team for penetrating analysis and for contributing to its conclusions and recommendations. In addition, any member may be called upon to counsel the entire team on points or questions which arise in his special field. Team members should not receive any directions or "directed verdict" relative to the survey, from management or persons outside the survey team. However, if such are received, they should be promptly and thoroughly reported to the project manager.

*Consultants*

A team may use internal consultants from the organization under study, or elsewhere in the company, to provide special knowledge or background on points or parts of a study. Such consultants may be requested to advise with the team on a particular part of the survey and thus may assist in formulating final recommendations pertaining to this portion. Consultants, as well as team members, should not discuss findings, conclusions, or recommendations pertaining to the survey with persons outside the survey team, without the prior knowledge and concurrence of the project manager.

*Availability of team members*

The project manager will consult with management to determine availability of survey-team candidates, and request in writing their assignment to the team for the period required.

*Team indoctrination*

Prior to the first meeting of the members, the project manager will plan a program for team indoctrination. This will include discussion of the objectives, the methods to be used, assignment of individuals to specific segments of the study (if necessary), and presentation of pertinent background information he has assembled from previous studies, correspondence, preliminary discussions with management, organization charts, management guides, job descriptions, and the like. If appropriate, he will arrange for management members to meet with the team during the indoctrination period to enlighten them on current management objectives, special problems, policies, and other pertinent matters. They utilize the job outline [Exhibit 10] to guide their work.

*Questionnaires*

In the event that it is decided too use questionnaires during the survey, the project manager will direct their preparation and will transmit them to the management of the organization to be studied, for distribution at the appropriate time to personnel to be interviewed. The transmittal should specify that questionnaires are to be completed by designated employees without consultation with fellow employees or their supervisors, and that the questionnaires should be retained by employees for discussion only with survey-team members. All employees' questionnaire replies are kept completely confidential from persons outside the survey team.

EXHIBIT 10. *Outlines used by department on organization to collect job information (Standard Oil Company of California).*

---

### Job outline

1. Describe the scope of your job. List plants, units, or area.
2. List your practical significant duties and approximate percent of time on each. (List these in sequence of their importance.)
3. From whom do you receive supervision?
4. What kind of supervision is received, and how frequently?
5. What unclassified and classified jobs do you supervise or give work direction to?
6. State type and frequency of this supervision or work direction. Also, about how many hours per day do you spend supervising (*a*) unclassified employees? (*b*) classified employees?

7. What agencies or organizations outside your division do you contact? Describe the nature and frequency of business.
8. List meetings you attend, how frequently, and normal time required.
9. What are your limits of authority for (*a*) ordering technical or other services? (*b*) changes in schedule or plans? (*c*) ordering maintenance, equipment, materials, or supplies? (*d*) personnel, and labor relations? (*e*) other?
10. List any other pertinent aspects of your job that have not been covered above, if any.
11. List any suggestions you may have for improvement and/or economies in your division or elsewhere in the refinery.

*Outline question No.*           Job Outline Supplement

1
1. Does the scope of your job change from time to time?
2. In your opinion, is the scope of your job too large, to small, or just right?
3. If too large or too small, how would you suggest correcting the situation?

2
1. Should any of these duties be eliminated?
2. Could some other division, organization, or agency better handle any of these duties?
3. Are there any duties you do not have which you think you should have?

3
1. Who provides counsel on your own personal matters such as salary changes, change in vacations, personal leave?
2. Do you receive occasional supervision from anyone not listed? Describe circumstances.

4
1. Do you receive too much, too little, or just the right amount of supervision?
2. If too much or too little, how could this be altered to improve the situation?

5, 6
1. Are you the only supervisor of this group? Who else provides supervision?
2. Does this group require your work direction after the normal day shift? And with what frequency? Nature of calls?
3. What is your frequency of being on call?

7
1. Should any of these contacts be eliminated?
2. Should any other division, organization, or agency handle any of these contacts?
3. Could any of these contacts be handled in a more efficient manner?

8
1. Do you consider any of these meetings a waste of time?

*General Activities and Organization Planning* 105

      2. Is your participation in all these meetings necessary?
      3. Could any of these meetings be eliminated and the same information distributed in some other manner, with no reduction in effective communication?
      4. Are all meetings well organized?
      5. How could any of these meetings be improved?
      6. Do you prepare any written reports? Are these regular, or intermittent? How much of your time does preparation of these reports require?

9    1. Are you handicapped in any way on your job by the limits of your authority?
      2. Can you suggest any changes in these limits?
      3. How much authority do you have within your plant, units, area? (*a*) to change operating conditions? (*b*) to change catalyst? (*c*) to shut down for maintenance? (*d*) to shut down for minor repair? (*e*) to change service of equipment such as tanks, lines, etc.? (*f*) to change manpower requirements? (*g*) to hire or fire? (*h*) to handle union grievance meetings?
      4. Does anyone preempt your authority?

*Job logs*

If job logs are to be used, careful consideration should be given to the type of information to be logged. Since job logging is time-consuming, useless or unnecessary job logging should be avoided. The project manager will transmit required forms to the unit being surveyed, with adequate instructions, including specification of the logging period.

*Advance communication*

The project manager will request that the management of the organization to be studied inform its employees of the survey and its general objectives; ask their cooperation; answer questions; and ask them to suggest any ideas they have for improvements. He will obtain, for the use of the team, copies of current organization charts, numbers of employees by classification in each organization unit, and lists of all men by name, shift, and vacation schedules.

---

    Then the field work begins. Interview and questionnaire methods predominate. The process of organization analysis seeks to answer the following questions:
    1. How essential is this (organization, unit, job, activity, function, procedure, product, process, or report)? What would happen if it were eliminated altogether?

2. If it is essential, what are its specific purposes or necessary objectives? What, specifically, does it seek to achieve?

3. What are the minimum functions necessary for people and machines to perform in order that these purposes or objectives will be achieved?

4. What are the methods, procedures, or techniques by which people and machines can best perform these minimum necessary functions? This is methods analysis, which itself has many variations.

5. How can these necessary functions so performed be best grouped into jobs, each constituting a reasonable workload for one person to accomplish? This involves grouping similar functions within human capacities, and workload analysis.

6. How many such performance-level jobs can reasonably be assigned to one supervisor to boss, how many such supervisors can report to one manager, and so on up the organizational hierarchy? This is organization-structure planning, with its own set of principles of grouping like functions, specialists versus generalists, span of control, direct and functional relationships, and so on.

7. What guidance does this organization need to function most effectively? This question may only prove the degree of management or executive direction which the head of the organization needs, or it may range throughout all levels of the organization and into such areas as the need for new or different corporation policies.

8. What administrative devices does this organization need? This may involve job descriptions, tables of authorities, communications guides, compensation plans, personnel procedures, and so on. At higher levels, it may involve the creation of new companies with many ramifications.

9. What forms of control are necessary, and how are they best achieved? At lower levels, this question is often partly or entirely answered in question 7; but for major units, control devices can be complex.

10. How is the success or failure of this unit to be judged? This is at the border line between organization and management. However, if organization planners have done their work well, success or failure will be evident and hard to hide.

Finally, this survey team leaves the field, prepares its recommendations and reports, and transmits them to management. Follow-up studies are often made.

This department consists of 25 full-time employees, about one half of whom are performing organization functions covered in preceding paragraphs. The others work in the field of compensation on a companywide basis. The department has found that, on the average, it takes a survey man one day for each individual in the organization being considered if a full-scale study of manpower, methods, procedures, and organization is required. As Frank Piersol, the department head, pointed out:

> It is absolutely essential that the organization department report directly to the chief executive. There can be no screening or filtering—it cannot work in any other way—there must be a close relationship if the department is to be effective. We are in constant contact with key executives of the company, constantly stimulating line management to minimize manpower and costs and maximize profitability. We are careful to remember our staff role. We never question line management's evaluation of people. We only review proposals to determine if they are within basic policy; we go back to the field or line management if there are doubts or questions, and generally we get agreement.

> We play an objective role in reviewing organization and manpower changes. We outline relationships and interfaces—how people work together, and who should make decisions. For new organizations, a very careful job of defining the tasks and key interfaces must be done.

Again, the pattern is clear; the emphasis of the department is on structural analysis and control of manpower. The department at Standard Oil of California is an organization-planning department par excellence.

## REFERENCES

1. Carlos Efferson, "Organization Planning for Management Growth," *Management Record* (April 1958), p. 134.

2. William F. Glueck, "Organization Development Departments in Selected American Firms: An Exploratory Behavioral Analysis" (Ph.D dissertation, Michigan State University, Ann Arbor, 1966). Published under the title, "Where Organization Planning Stands Today," *Personnel* (July–August 1967), pp. 19–26.

# 5. Organization Development and Combined Activities

ORGANIZATION development emphasizes the integration of structural factors with human factors. Executives who use this approach tend to believe that an organization cannot be analyzed without considering both the attitudes and the orientations of the persons concerned, and the working environment that has evolved as the organization has grown. Some business authorities believe that organizations develop personalities and lives of their own, existing independent of the executives and employees working in them. Such a climate sometimes develops because of policies or values of strong executives who had roles of leadership in the company's earlier years. These executives impressed their management style and policies on behavior norms, hiring practices, benefits, and the like, which are still reflected in the attitudes and work of persons in the organization. Attempting to apply universal principles of organization without considering the company work climate is a disservice to the organization process.

Another important factor is that people differ. Their opinions vary widely about how superiors and subordinates should behave; therefore, the application of organization analysis uniformly throughout a company without considering behavioral and environment variables is unlikely to produce sound results, in the opinion of many advocates of organization development.

Of course, there are varying degrees of emphasis. Some organization planners do consider both people and environment, even though their statements of objectives, job activities, and opinions do not provide evidence of major emphasis on these variables. In general, advocates of organization development are more likely to emphasize integration of structural, behavioral, and environmental variables when they come to grips with organization problems.

## Operating Patterns of Organization Development

Organization development in action was described by executives in several participating companies. Since numerous details were needed to provide a complete picture of the departments' operating patterns, vice-presidents discussed the many factors that shaped the establishment, development, and implementation of the function in their companies.

### UniRoyal, Incorporated

William Wrightnour, vice-president, personnel, of UniRoyal, explained the establishment of organization development in his company as follows: "We started the organization function in 1958 because we wanted to gradually change the whole character of the company and the way we had been organized, including the organization structure and the people in it."

Mr. Wrightnour emphasized that the organization function must have a frame of reference in which to operate, adding, "you cannot organize a corporation in a vacuum—without some objective in mind. If you try to do so, you find you are engaged merely in organization maintenance. Even reorganizing people is not organization work, as I see it. What you have to keep in mind in your objectives is change."

The president of UniRoyal, George Vila, with the help of Mr. Wrightnour and other top-level executives, plans for the work environment, the people in the organization, and the organization structure. Mr. Wrightnour described several of these activities:

One of the nice things about being a large company is that we can have several experimental units going. We're organizing one unit one way, and another a different way, to get some experience. We took our Canadian organization because it was an integrated unit, and reorganized it entirely. We started to lose ground the first year, but we are now coming out; and that pattern has helped us learn how to organize our British operation.

Not long ago we made a change in one division of the company that upset its personnel terribly. For 75 years it had always had a marketing man for division manager, because marketing was the great emphasis in this particular division. But the new manager had a Ph.D. in chemistry. The division by itself would not have made such a change. It is something the boss (Mr. Vila) did after very careful thought. It involves a calculated risk, because the switch-over is going to cost us something.

As a matter of fact, the division had been slipping because it had not been able to adapt quickly enough to the new materials and processes, largely chemical in nature, that are going to be its salvation. We may have convinced people in the division that they don't have to use rubber when they can use a plastic, and that they can do a few other things that they haven't been doing. One thing we don't want to do, for example, is to repeat our performance as the largest producers of garden hose. We produced ourselves right out of the business and into a big red figure because the people doing it thought that garden hose should never be made of anything but cotton and rubber. And, of course, you know what happened to the garden-hose business: It became a plastics business.

So organization changes must be made to build-in changes in people and environment, along with structural changes.

Such decisions must be made at UniRoyal's corporate headquarters, rather than in the divisions, said Mr. Wrightnour, because divisions will not make some types of changes. He explained:

We found that divisions will not reorganize themselves into or out of a business. They will not organize themselves to keep abreast of new developments, because it is a most difficult thing to change. That is why top management with long-range plans must take the lead in planning the organization. And that is why a change of presidents is sometimes needed. Many feel that their responsibility is largely a custodial one. They don't intend to stick their necks out.

We're an old company. For years, we were the volume leader in the rubber industry. Then we saw our business change from first in sales to third. One of the reasons was that we had some executives acting as custodians. They were living in the past and were not willing to take the risk to go all-out. So the company chose to elect as president a man who was willing to put his reputation on the line and run the risk of being fired by the board of directors, because he was going to reverse the trend.

After studying the situation, the one thing that we felt we must do to turn the business around was to get our hands on a key resource—manpower—all aspects of manpower. We had to work on all the problems of an old organization with its obsolescent practices. We had to do some very tough things in personnel administration. For example, we sometimes passed over people when making promotions, and we broke down old traditions concerning job security.

As a matter of fact, about five years ago I began to feel we were making some headway when I had a young fellow quit after being with us a year. He said he had joined UniRoyal originally because it was traditional that you had security if you had a job with the company—but he was now seeing definite evidence that merit rather than service determined the security of the job.

## Mr. Wrightnour sees organization's responsibilities as

One, to set policy. We decide what policy is going to be. Two, we suggest preferred procedures; but we don't care what a division or unit does, as long as it doesn't violate policy. Three—and a big one—is control. This is where we differ from many companies, because they say that corporate staff is advisory. But we don't limit our role to advising.

There appears to be a considerably different approach to organization work at UniRoyal, as compared with companies that use the organization-planning approach. UniRoyal formally integrated and acted on the analysis and change of the people working in the organization, the work environment the company desired, and the appropriate organization structure—primarily on the structural side of analysis and change.

## Electro-Optical Systems Division, Xerox Corporation

Electro-Optical was formerly a rapidly growing entrepreneurial firm that had reached a point where it could no longer be managed by one man. It had to be converted into a managerial firm. After clarification of the top management positions (separating operations from planning, organization, and control), goals were set. The organization plan was developed around the values of the former president, Sandy Sigaloff, who explained during the research for this study:

The most difficult thing for me was the development of a creed. My values about organization environment had to be put into the organization and then molded around the organization. Very quickly, we came up with a five-point creed which indicates my personal values.

1. *Firm belief in the dignity of the individual.* Corporations which say the business is first and the family is second are naïve, because the family is first, and will always be first, to responsible people. What you try to do is build a sense of proportion between the obligations of the corporation and its desire to be an enterprise, and the recognition of the importance of the man to his family.

2. *Pride.* This is personal responsibility in daily activity. You have to be proud of your job, and have to make other people feel proud.

3. *Quality.* Since this is a technology-oriented company, the difference between us and anybody else is response time and quality.

4. *Accountability,* to the lowest possible level within the organization. Anybody can make a mistake, but he has to recognize that in making that mistake he must bring it to his supervisor's attention rapidly enough for correction.

5. *Venture spirit.* We said we would be moderately aggressive. In other words, we would make profits as we grow; we would not grow and then hope to have the profits fill the vacuum.

Mr. Sigaloff described how organization followed the development of a creed into a work environment:

The next thing was to build the organization into a team. I happen to believe in teams, and also believe that there can only be one leader on a team. Every player on the team must know with extreme precision what is expected of him at every time, the full range of his responsibilities, the full range of his authority, and the full range of the risks that he controls. He doesn't have to agree with the basic policy. But he has to implement his portion of it to perfection and recognize that if he fails, we all suffer. He cannot be a yes man, but he must understand that with the right to disagree goes the acceptance of a policy, once it is decided.

We next went through a very difficult selection policy, since we had to find the quality of man we wanted. We knew we would never find the optimum. The question was how we could take the best features, make those features do the job as a team member, and play down the negatives that everybody has.

Having done all this, we were ready to work on organization. There was a stated and defined policy of building the organization with the people inside the corporation, not going outside. Of course, this meant taking men who might be in the wrong job. The man who is the general manager may not know how to do his job, but could run a small empire as an autocrat. O.K., we have to move him; and retrain him.

Mr. Sigaloff said that the organization-development process involved retraining many people and rewarding those who succeeded. Organization development also helped interpret corporate policy, served as a feedback device, and helped integrate the environment—with change of organization structure and people. He added that organization development changed as the nature of the firm changed. As the firm diversified, the process changed; as it spread out, the process of organization called for other changes. In the future, as the company further diversifies and becomes more geographically dispersed, organization development should become even more an integral part of the corporate-planning process.

Donald Taffi, former vice-president, organization, explained that the function at Electro-Optical was participating in a series of related projects to implement the president's vision.

We got ourselves involved in value studies of the individual, and in trying to identify motivational aspects and finding out why a man wants to move into a specific area of management. You can't separate that from the job. Most scientists, for example, want to move into management because they think it carries with it prestige and financial remuneration. It also has one other attraction. Scientists move into management because they can do what they want to do, which is primarily technical contribution, and they can delegate their management responsibility. And this is where we get into a great deal of trouble. Often the individual to whom they delegate this responsibility is an administrative assistant who has managed a laboratory but lacks managerial competence.

Mr. Taffi spent about 90 percent of his time with top management, serving as adviser on the organization-development process. He helped the firm implement the organization process and sense the need for change, and served as a source of feedback to the president.

Again, the pattern emerges of concern and action in more than organization-structure analysis and change. It is involvement in developing and implementing plans to maximize results and satisfaction of employees by integrating environmental factors, structure, and other organizational factors, and people's abilities and attitudes—meanwhile taking into consideration the overall strategy of the business.

*Kaiser Aluminum and Chemical Corporation*

At Kaiser, the vice-president in charge of the department of organization was Dr. Carlos Efferson, whose writings on this subject cover a period of ten years and whose experience covers a much longer period. Kaiser's president, T. J. Ready, works directly with Dr. Efferson on a number of organizational matters.

The vice-president spent about 3 percent of his time on long-range organization planning and 10 percent on developing an ideal organization structure for Kaiser, without reference to the people in it. But 87 percent of his time was devoted to creating, for top management, an integrated organization that involved a meshing of people, structure, and environment. This included the implementation of the company's organization plan. Dr. Efferson was assisted in his work by a team of specialists which included an organization counsel, supervising organization analyst, senior organization analyst, and organization specialist. (See position description in Exhibit 11.)

EXHIBIT 11. *Position description of director of organization planning (Kaiser Aluminum and Chemical Corporation).*

---

*Primary purpose of position*

Responsible to recommend, implement, and coordinate objectives, policies, and plans related to organization, organization structure, and organization relationships; assist in the establishment of management-manpower requirements.

*Duties and responsibilities*

Responsible to:
1. Implement the development and maintenance of sound, clear-cut plans of organization, under which headquarters and field management can most effectively direct, coordinate, and control their assigned objectives.
2. Determine the source and cause of organization problems. Compare similar or analogous allocations of functions, responsibilities, and authority, as they might cast light on corrective measures.
3. Determine functions, define their duties and responsibilities, insure complete coverage, eliminate overlapping authority, and logically group them into appropriate departmental classifications.
4. Coordinate planning and measurement aspects with organization, insofar as they impinge upon the effectiveness of organization planning.
5. Form and guide appropriate committee actions aimed at organization planning, structuring, and implementing.
6. Maintain joint responsibility, with other departments involved, in the proper coordination of organization structure with available and potential management-manpower capabilities.
7. Develop and review appropriate position descriptions as their content bears

# Organization Development and Combined Activities 115

upon the assignment of duties and responsibilities consistent with the organization plan in question.
8. Insure that proper delegation of authority permits decisions to be made at the lowest practicable level of management.
9. Insure the development and maintenance of appropriate organization manuals.
10. Insure that policy statements are coordinated, when multiple departments or functions are involved.
11. Assist in the development and maintenance of appropriate policy manuals.
12. Review appropriate practice and procedure manuals for conformity with assigned responsibilities.
13. Periodically review, and continually adjust and keep current, the various plans of organization.
14. Project the various organizations into the future, in terms of desired objectives and developing personnel.
15. Keep abreast of the latest developments in organization planning and related fields, including, too, the standing of our competitors.

---

Dr. Efferson spoke enthusiastically about his job:

Assisting Kaiser Aluminum plan for the future is a unique professional experience. Helping a company to articulate objectives—the basis of planning—is not unique. Nor is it unusual for one to help design organization structure to accomplish these objectives. What is unique is trying to do these things in a way that capitalizes most on the most valuable assets of Kaiser Aluminum.

For we began by inheriting a living legend—in more ways than one—from our relentless founder–chairman. Of all the reasons one could gather to account for his successes, two stand out with clarity and certainty. First, he selected good men who were ambitious, conscientious, dedicated, and who wanted a chance to work hard and grow. And, second, he gave them responsibility of the broadest kind, which carried with it the expectation that each man would have a feeling of personal accountability for the business.

His rule of thumb for developing good managers has been to throw a good man in over his head and let him swim to the top. The good men came willingly, and Mr. Kaiser provided plenty of deep water.

This process developed a "Kaiser spirit" with its fun of achievement, limitless opportunity, sweat, and dedication. It has developed people of broad and mature business capabilities and self-confidence.

Dr. Efferson described how organization planning at Kaiser began with discussions with the then president and vice-president:

In 1956 Mr. Rhoades and Mr. Ready began talking with me about an organization plan to insure the retention of our most valuable assets in the fast-changing and increasingly complex environment of our company, our industry, and American business. We were sure that we had good people, as good as managers anywhere; but our forecast of growth showed that it would be more and more difficult, with our centralized organization structure, for these good men to operate in the independent, responsibility-for-a-whole-business way that is indispensable for the development of the most mature and able kind of management leadership.

## Dr. Efferson explained the evolution of the Kaiser organization:

From our beginning until 1957, Kaiser Aluminum was functionally organized—that is, it had one head of all sales and one head of all production. This is a most effective and economical organization structure, up to a certain point in the growth and complexity of a business. It had served us well. However, as we forecast the product lines, markets, sales volume, nature of competition in the years ahead, and additional opportunities here and abroad, it became clearly evident that a different kind of structure was needed for the future.

Mr. Rhoades said at the time: "We must be organized so that I can turn to just one person when there's a question on any major product or market. This one person and his people must live and breathe this one major product line and market. More people should have experience in making the same types of decisions Mr. Ready and I have to make—that is, broad business decisions or profit-center decisions. The whole structure should not only make continued growth possible; it must compel it through the next 10, 20, and up to 50 years. I want an organization structure that will give our best managers a feeling of complete responsibility for a complete segment of our business, a segment large enough to challenge to the fullest, but small enough for them to handle. I want them to feel the same challenge and responsibility and esprit de corps that all of us felt in 1946 when Kaiser Aluminum got its start."

The only possible way to accomplish these objectives is through some form of divisionalization.

## Dr. Efferson continued:

For more than six months, a diversified team of us studied our company, its products, its customers, and its long-range future. We studied the basic business first—the domestic operations. In July 1957 we split our aluminum business into five divisions and several subdivisions, each with responsibility for production, sales, and supporting staff (profit responsibility). As anticipated, this major step created some new problems of coordination, but individual managers with personal accountability had been placed in charge of manageable segments and were solving problems like those with which any company president must deal.

The results within the aluminum operations have been far greater than even the most optimistic of us was willing to project in 1957.

We then turned attention to other opportunities. Refractories, our second major product line, were part of the organization in 1946 and were always operated as a separate entity apart from the aluminum business. Refractories had been the "chemicals"—somewhat inaccurately named—of Kaiser Aluminum and Chemical Corporation. As a result of steady growth in our refractories business, and merger with Mexico Refractories Company, these operations now accounted for 10 percent of our business. Refractories are inherently independent of aluminum operations and deserve a degree of independence comparable to that enjoyed by a separate company. Although legally it is a major division, we call it Kaiser Refractories Company.

But we were still in the chemicals business in other ways, as a result of our integrated aluminum production, and wanted to grow still further in selected parts of this giant industry. Simultaneously, with the announcement of construction of our fluorocarbon facility in Louisiana, steps were taken to set our chemical business out as a separate company-like operation, since its markets are inherently separate from both aluminum and refractories.

Finally, we had made such progress in international sales and operations that this business likewise needed exclusive top management direction and identity as a separate company to insure its objective for leadership in the international market. So today Kaiser Aluminum and Chemical Corporation, though basically an aluminum company, is an organization of four companies—*aluminum, refractories, chemicals,* and *international.*

From the major reorganization in the late 1950s to the present, Dr. Efferson has been engaged in significant activities for the corporation. A partial list of his major projects in the course of one year substantiates the extent of his involvement:

1. Helping develop the roles and relationships in the pollution-control department.
2. Organizing the legal department.
3. Developing effective relations between patent department and line operations.
4. Reorienting corporate staff from primary concern for domestic operations to an international outlook.
5. Analyzing the relationships between personnel relations and labor relations—how they can be more effectively integrated and coordinated.
6. Utilizing the computer in an integrated management information system.

7. Defining effective roles and relationships of planning groups at corporate, division, and department levels.
8. Determining the amount of authority for capital analysis and requirements to be delegated to divisions.
9. Analyzing supply and distribution operations of the company.
10. Clarifying the role of the aluminum division's international department's staff and the aluminum manager's staff.

Carlos Efferson is deeply involved in the framework for organization development—the planning of the business objectives for Kaiser. As he says, "Planning has become the vehicle on which the company rides." The company planned and created divisionalization that involved profit responsibility for the marketing managers. The divisions became product-oriented profit centers—"separate businesses"—with managers held accountable for performance against objectives, not merely against results in earnings.

Thus organization development at Kaiser attempts to integrate the Kaiser spirit, its people, and their abilities and attitudes, into organization analysis and change. The analysis and change themselves are important, but they are also an integral part of total analysis: structure, people, environment.

*Two Development Techniques*

Two methods that have been developed by organization-development specialists are the "Managerial Grid" of Robert Blake and Jane Mouton[1] and the "Management Responsibility Guide" of Robert Melcher.[2] Mr. Blake and Mrs. Mouton have developed a technique based on different leadership styles to achieve the goal of organization development, which they define as follows: "to increase operational effectiveness by increasing the degree of integration of the seven properties of organization. Three of the seven properties are critical for development. They are purpose, human interaction, and organization culture."

These specialists have developed a six-phase approach around their managerial grid. Phase 1 provides an explanation of the grid; phases 2 and 3 move into team development and intergroup development. Phase 4 involves building a model of the ideal organization; phase 5, implementing this model; and Phase 6, stabilizing the new organization.

Robert Melcher's management responsibility guide deals with two of the most difficult problems in organization development: (1) providing a mechanism to systematically and objectively describe the managerial job to be done, (2) involving members of the work group in clarifying and resolving their interpersonal and intergroup role and relationship differences.

The organization consultant helps management develop a common focal point for resolving differences by objectively defining, in a systems context, the managerial functions that need to be performed to meet each work group's objectives. Once agreement is reached by the work group's supervisor and each subordinate, the functions are entered on the management responsibility guide matrix format. Then the manager and supervisor enter on this form what they think are the required relationships for each position according to the management responsibility relationship codes described in following paragraphs.

*General responsibility.* Individual guides and directs execution of function through the person delegated operating responsibility, and has approval authority over function.

*Operating responsibility.* Individual is directly responsible, at the operating level, for execution of function.

*Specific responsibility.* Individual is delegated responsibility for executing specific or limited portion of function.

*Must be consulted.* Individual must be called in prior to any decision made, or approval granted, to confer, render advice, or relate information, but does not make decision or grant approval.

*Must be notified.* Individual must be notified of action that has been taken.

*Must approve.* Individual (other than persons holding general and operating responsibility) must grant approval.

After agreements have been reached about the relationships, data are entered on the management responsibility guide (Exhibit 12).

The organization-development specialist next involves members of the work group in a discussion so they can resolve differences in

EXHIBIT 12. *Management responsibility guide.*

| | | Management Position | | | | | | | | |
|---|---|---|---|---|---|---|---|---|---|---|
| Number | Function | | Relationship code | A General responsibility | B Operating responsibility | C Specific responsibility | D Must be consulted | E May be consulted | F Must be notified | G Must approve |

| Organization identification | Number | Approval: | Date | Page No. ___ of ___ |

© R. Melcher, 1967

perception. He helps them to change attitudes and to plan changes for the environment and organization structure to fit their decisions. Once differences are resolved within a work group, they can be resolved between the work group and other groups.

## Combined Activities

The difference between organization planning or development departments and joint departments is one of emphasis. A separate organization department may perform some other functions, but most of its people are specialists. In a joint department, a large majority of the employees are usually specialists in other fields, and a small number of organization specialists form a subdivision of the department. The typical combinations include organization as part of personnel or industrial relations, corporate planning, or administration. Of the 59 joint departments of companies participating in this study, 81 percent (48) include organization in personnel departments, 10 percent (6) in corporate planning, 7 percent (4) in administration, and 2 percent (one company) in another activity.

The joint departments are usually found in medium-size and, to a lesser extent, smaller firms. In many of these firms, the departments combine organization with the following functions:

- Corporate personnel, including recruitment, development, wage and salary administration, and medical and safety services.
- Corporate industrial relations, including labor contractors, personnel policies, wage and salary administration, and recruitment of key personnel.
- Labor relations, employment, training and development, safety, workmen's compensation and public liability claims (in a self-insured company), and wage and salary administration.
- College recruiting, and hiring technical and professional employees.
- Employment and recruiting, training, communications, safety, wage and salary administration, personnel records, employee benefit planning, and administration.
- Employment, training and development, wage and salary administration, personnel services, and office services.
- Public relations and administrative services.
- Administration of corporate-planning activity; long-range planning;

marketing research; long-range marketing and product-planning coordination.
- All long-range planning; plans for marketing, facilities, finance, and systems, and their coordination and administration into corporate plan; also, new product introduction planning and coordination.
- Overall corporate planning, market research.

Examples of policies of joint departments are provided for some of the combinations listed.

*Organization and Personnel*

In one diversified manufacturing company, organization is a functional subdivision of the personnel department. This arrangement was explained by the company as follows:

In setting down the function and objectives of the personnel department, recognition is given to the fact that the line organization is, in the final analysis, responsible for the day-by-day administration of personnel matters and the effective utilization of the people in the organization. The personnel department, as a specialized staff group, has the responsibility of assisting and giving guidance to the line organization in the execution of its responsibilities in the area of personnel and manpower management.

This department has the following primary responsibilities: (1) to assist company management in the formulation of objectives, plans, policies, and procedures relating to the maximum effective and enlightened use of the human resources of the company; (2) to carry on a continuing study, analysis, and evaluation of all aspects of the company's personnel program, leading to concrete recommendations to management concerning the program; (3) to assist in the interpretation of management policies to employees, and employees' points of view and attitudes to management; (4) to assist in every way possible all those who direct the work of others in their efforts to become more effective in the area of personnel and manpower management; (5) to perform for the line organization that work related to personnel administration which can best be performed on a centralized basis.

The organization unit within the department has the following objectives, listed in the order of their importance:

## Organization

To study and analyze on a continuing basis the organizational relationships with respect to function, responsibilities, authorities, and titles, and to recommend effective organizational structures based on the results of such studies.

To maintain in current form organization charts down through department and division level so that each unit will be informed of its function and its relationship with the functions of other units in the company organization.

To work toward the end of having for each position a position description which outlines the responsibilities that must be carried out if the position is to function properly in the integrated organization structure.

To further work toward the end of having for each position a position specification indicating the requirements to be sought in the person filling the position as an aid in recruitment, placement, and training and development.

## Work measurement and staff control

To continually study the work units of the company toward the goal of cost reduction and cost control through the techniques of work elimination, work simplification, and work measurement.

To effect these cost savings with accompanying higher service levels and increased individual and unit efficiency.

To maintain a positive and effective control over staff size through work measurement reports and organizational analysis procedures.

To project annually the staff requirements on both a short-term (one year) and long-term (five to ten years) basis, and to make plans for meeting the needs indicated. In determining the staff requirements, consideration should be given to both the numbers and the specifications of individuals necessary to meet these requirements.

## Recruitment, selection, and placement

To develop, through personal contact and the distribution of appropriate literature, the prestige of the insurance industry and of our company as a career opportunity in order that we may attract a sufficient number of the right kind of applicants for employment.

To carry out all recruiting and selection activities in such a manner as to foster the best in public relations with recruiting sources, applicants, and other persons or organizations.

To select, without prejudice concerning race, color, religion, sex, age, or national origin, the persons best qualified to fill our employment needs.

To seek out persons with imagination, creative ability, and aggressiveness, and to use these qualities as primary factors in selection in order that we may have the dynamic organization necessary to implement the company objectives.

To be familiar with the requirements of the various positions throughout the company so that selection and placement can be made on the basis of best matching the employee's interests and abilities to the requirements of the job.

*Training and development*

To properly indoctrinate new employees with the traditions, philosophies, and practices of the company through an initial, centralized orientation program and continuing efforts carried on within the departmental areas.

To assist in the preparation and implementation of programs and courses designed to enable all employees to receive the training necessary to perform their present positions satisfactorily and to progress to positions of greater responsibility.

## Organization and Corporate Planning

A large insurance company integrates organization with corporate planning. The vice-president of corporate planning in this firm explained the scope of his department in these words:

> The total planning responsibility for the company, including organization planning, is in our department. Our particular assignment is to identify the organizational problems and come up with an organizational plan. These problems are related to the objectives of the firm and the business that we are in. We integrate organization planning, business planning, and market planning into the corporate-planning process.

## Organization and Administration

Administration departments vary considerably in American companies. In many firms they include departments for computer services and corporate legal departments. In smaller firms, they sometimes include the personnel department. The example given, that of a medium-size metals company, is therefore not presented as a typical administration department. However, it is one way that organization can be part of an administration department.

The company's management is divided into the following functional areas: marketing and planning, manufacturing, research and engineering, the secretary's office, and administration. Administration includes the following activities:

# Organization Development and Combined Activities

- Administrative organization development and organization planning.
- Personnel relations and administration, and labor relations.
- Manpower planning, management-succession planning, and employee and training development.
- Systems and procedures.
- Management improvement, management performance standards, and administrative work measurement and work simplification.
- Wage and salary administration, executive compensation, and incentive plans.
- Group insurance benefit programs, safety, suggestion systems, and memberships and subscriptions.
- Community relations, employee communication, and clearance of speeches and talks.
- Forms and reports control, records retention, office supply and equipment standards, reproduction services and equipment, and communications (mechanical).

In fulfilling its organization responsibilities, the unit is involved in organization change. Company policy on this calls for the following procedure:

1. Changes in A-type positions, involving personnel organization or reporting relationships, will be made in accordance with the following steps:
    A. Local approval procedures will be completed.
    B. The plan for change will be submitted to the vice-president, administration, who will (*a*) notify the appropriate corporate functional vice-president; (*b*) arrange for required review and decision steps; and (*c*) notify divisions of approval or disapproval, as appropriate.
2. While not mandatory for changes in minor positions, the steps outlined are recommended.

The function operates within a framework of principles of management (Exhibit 13) and principles of organization (Exhibit 14).

EXHIBIT 13. *Principles of management (medium-size metals company).*

---

Policy

Decentralization of management

Management is decentralized to the extent that the delegation of authority and responsibility for results is at that level in the organization where decisions about an activity can be made on the basis of adequate and timely knowledge and understanding of the important facts, and where the realization of the maximum economies accrues to the company as a whole. In this respect some activities are more efficiently performed at the corporate level, and others more efficiently at the division, subsidiary, or plant level. However, the requirements of decentralization may shift from one level of management to another as deemed desirable by the changing demands of operations.

Management controls

Strong controls are developed and applied by all levels of management through meaningful objectives, policies, and procedures. This requires preplanned action, timely information about significant variations, timely follow-up, and timely adjustments to meet changing conditions.

Performance measurements

Effective standards are developed and maintained so that the performance of any manager or supervisor can be properly measured and evaluated, and their efforts coordinated with the needs of the business.

Use of committees

There are sound reasons for using committees to supplement and coordinate management and staff activities. Their judicious use is encouraged. However, a committee cannot assume authority or responsibility for decision, action, or results. The chairman alone is responsible and accountable. A committee serves only in an advisory capacity to the chairman.

Members of corporate, division, subsidiary, or plant committees must act individually in making their recommendations, and support that action most advantageous to the organization as a whole. The effect of this on their assigned area of responsibility is of only secondary importance.

Personal challenge

The delegation of authority and responsibility must provide for sufficient scope of opportunity and challenge in the job of every management employee.

Restrictions on delegation of authority and responsibility

Authority not expressed and in writing, reserved to higher levels of management through policies, procedures, and directives, etc., is granted to lower levels of management. If a question arises regarding the delegation of authority, it must be referred to the next higher level of management for clarification.

Delegation of authority and responsibility

Managers and supervisors must be concerned with the important aspects of their position; and delegate, to the maximum extent, detail and routine matters. The delegation of authority must be consistent with the delegation of responsibility.

However, delegation does not divest the one in higher authority of ultimate responsibility. No member of management can disassociate himself from the acts of his subordinates. He is as responsible as they are for what is done or is not done.

Establishment of organizational units

As many organizational units as are necessary to efficiently transact the business may be established. The basic pattern of organization may call for management by function, geographic location, product, or some combination of these. A key consideration in this respect, however, is to avoid creating units of a size incapable of supporting a management team of sufficient quality and quantity. In addition, a proper balance must be established and maintained, including product assignments as well as growth potential, between the various units.

Relationships between organizational units

The relationships between corporate, division, subsidiary, and plant units are always conducted so that maximum benefits accrue to the company as a whole. Close and friendly relations are maintained, but based strictly on the requirements of conducting operations in an efficient manner.

Communication of information

The free interchange of information, including recommendations, criticism, etc., must be encouraged by all management personnel. In this respect a primary objective is to provide for this interchange not only between positions at the same level, but from the top level down and from the bottom level up.

Objectives

To enhance the quality and speed of decision making by placing the responsibility for it as close as possible to the source of the results.

To outline the basic principles of company management.

---

EXHIBIT 14. *Principles of organization (medium-size metals company).*

---

Policy

General provisions

There are basic principles of organization planning observed in any well-managed organization. Management and supervisory personnel of the company must be familiar with these principles and apply them in an appropriate manner.

Type of organization

When a company is establishing a new organization, whether a division, plant, department, or other, the objectives and basic plans must be first determined, and then a structure designed to efficiently and economically carry them out.

The structure of the organization must be simple, with the number of levels kept to a minimum. Each additional level lengthens the chain of authority and responsibility and complicates the problems of communication and coordination.

The organization must be flexible enough to adapt readily to new and changing conditions either within or outside the company, and without disrupting the underlying structure.

The type of organization developed must permit every manager and supervisor to exercise maximum initiative within the limits of delegated authority.

Assignment of functional activities

A primary step in organization is to determine and to establish, as separate entities, the smallest number of dissimilar functions into which the work of the business may be divided. The nature and number of basic functions is determined by their relative importance in contributing directly to the purpose of the business.

Activities that are closely related or similar are placed under the same function.

Functional activities are established and assigned with due attention to proper balance in order to avoid overemphasis on the less important activities and underemphasis on the essential ones.

Line and staff activities are clearly defined and kept separate. In this respect, however, proper balance is provided for, between line and staff activities, to insure that the pressure of day-by-day operations does not interfere with essential planning work.

There must be no overlap, duplication, or conflict regarding the responsibility of positions in the organization for the performance, supervision, coordination, and control of activities.

Organization relationships

Employees reporting to one manager or supervisor are not to exceed the number that can be effectively supervised and coordinated.

No person reports to more than one supervisor. Every supervisor must know the persons who report to him, and every employee must know the person to whom he reports.

The plan of organization must permit and require the exercise of common sense and good judgment, at all levels, in determining the best channels of contact to expedite work. These channels are not described or limited by the lines of authority and responsibility of the organization structure. In making contact beyond the lines of authority and responsibility shown on an organization chart, it is the duty of each manager and supervisor to keep his senior informed on: (1) matters on which his senior may be held accountable; (2) matters in disagreement or likely to cause controversy within or between units of the organization; (3) matters requiring consideration by the senior, or coordination with other units of the organization; (4) matters involving recommendations for change in, or variance from, approved objectives, policies, and procedures.

Staff instructions to units under the supervision of others must be channeled through the responsible supervisors.

The working relationships between units of an organization and with outside organizations must be clearly defined and thoroughly understood by everyone concerned.

Objectives

To provide guides for the establishment and maintenance of an efficient organization.

To provide guides for the evaluation of new or revised organization plans.

## Joint Departments—A Conclusion

Joint or combined-function departments provide services similar to those of separate departments of organization. They tend to concentrate primarily on either organization planning or organization development. Depending on the size of the subunit and the orientation of the reporting department, they tend either to become submerged beneath the department's other staff services or to grow for the benefit of the corporation.

The organization unit of a combined department sometimes has its own organizational problems. Its status and usefulness tend to reflect the status of the larger department. For example, if organization is part of a personnel department and the personnel department is oriented to the blue collar worker or to records, or if it has a secondary role because top management is not people-oriented, the organization unit finds it difficult to perform key activities. Top managers are likely to believe the unit unable to deal with top management problems or major organization problems. If this happens, the function of organization is reduced to minor organization studies. When the organization section finds itself submerged by this type of situation, it may attempt to separate itself from the department.

But the reverse is also true. If personnel is a dynamic, well-regarded function because of its contributions to the company's activities, if it is headed by capable and influential executives, and if the president of the company is people-oriented, the organization section may have a very advantageous role in the department. Its contributions can then be enhanced and its usefulness magnified throughout the company.

### References

1. Robert Blake and Jane Mouton, "Grid Organization Development," *Personnel Administration,* January–February 1967, pp. 8–16.
2. Robert Melcher, "Roles and Relationships—Clarifying the Manager's Job," *Personnel,* May–June 1967, pp. 33–41.

# 6. Accomplishments and Challenges

PERHAPS the most difficult aspect of analyzing a staff service such as organization planning and development is the assessment of its value to the company. Yet most executives believe assessment is a useful exercise even though they realize that it is a far more difficult task than evaluating a line function. In the questionnaire survey conducted for this study, organization executives were asked to specify the most important accomplishment made by organization planning and development in the past few years. Company presidents were asked several questions about their evaluation of the function, and the workshop participants discussed this topic at length. In addition, all participants were encouraged to discuss the problems or difficulties they have experienced in organization planning and development.

### ACCOMPLISHMENTS OF PARTICIPATING COMPANIES

In response to the questionnaire item about major accomplishments, most organization executives gave brief answers. As would be expected, some responses were organization-planning accomplishments and some were organization-development accomplishments. However, a number of the others were primarily personnel-related.

Some of the organization-planning accomplishments that emphasize improvement or changes in the organization structure were reported as:

Development of clear delegations of authority for principal company executives. (Automobile company)

Assisting with the company's transition from a functional to a decentralized divisional organization structure; and assisting with the myriad and complex organizational problems involved in mergers. (Large oil company)

Conducting surveys, over the past three years, which have resulted in annual savings of $40 million. (Standard Oil Company of California)

Helping with a recent merger; consolidation of information services functions; recognition and centralization of facility and airport planning; strengthening of the operations-planning function; and maintenance of a consistent organization policy. (Major airline)

Another set of accomplishments fits into the organization-development pattern—a combination of attention to the structure and to the development of people and environment to help achieve organization goals. Some of these accomplishments cited by organization executives of participating companies are the following:

Gaining acceptance on the part of individual departments to plan for organization needs (structure and personnel) *before* the fact. Also, making some headway toward integrating these plans on a companywide basis. (Lukens Steel)

Greater recognition by all managers of the importance of organization to them. General acceptance of goals and objectives as a way of managing. Greatly strengthened corporate and divisional structure and management staff. (The Stanley Works)

Achievement of an environment conducive to long-range organization thinking and planning at the same level of importance and urgency as the other planning areas. (Samsonite)

Development of corporationwide compensation plans, key management replacement program, coordination of organization planning and development plans in divisions, and participation in several key reorganizations. (Sperry Rand)

Developing managerial compensation; developing and executing plans for expansion through organizational changes; developing improved communication by means of coordinating corporate staff and division staff functions. (Medium-size coal company)

Some departments—either joint-function or organization departments with a heavy personnel orientation—cited primary accomplishments that normally are achieved by personnel departments.

*Accomplishments and Challenges* 133

The installation of an effective management development effort. (W. R. Grace)

Development of a system to identify future managerial talent. (Pharmaceutical company)

Establishment of management performance appraisal and inventory program. (White Motor)

The establishment of personnel inventory manuals with organization replacement charts; a list of young, high-potential executives; executive inventory sheets; and management development requirements. (Kelsey-Hayes)

Helping influence management toward more liberal views on numerical reduction, training, and advancement of shorter-service employees. (Remington Arms)

Although these departments do perform organization activities, their primary accomplishments are people-oriented, with little emphasis on organization per se.

Detailed descriptions of organization planning and development accomplishments were provided by executives during interviews and in the workshop session. Their comments and explanations give additional insight and understanding of the department's role and working relationships.

## Bank of America

Organization specialists of Bank of America provided a typical example of their accomplishments: a study of the relationships of functional operations (central administration) to branch bank operations. These specialists' activities in conducting the study may be outlined briefly as follows:

1. Obtained agreement about what functions actually were.
2. Did field study, and talked to 68 of the 72 senior officers and 16 junior officers to determine how time was spent.
3. Found actual contact time was 22 hours per week clerical time and expense cost, or $1,758,000 to support 92 contact officers.
4. Explored alternative approaches.
5. Made recommendations to consolidate specialists and create generalists, and to realign geographic boundaries.
6. Evaluated degree of insulation, communications or distortion points, authorization of authority, and coordination.

7. Conducted pilot study in Sacramento, California, and found that change was successful.
8. Initiated new plan in other branches.
9. Completed change on statewide basis in 925 branches.

The bank emphasized that its organization planners are free agents and can deal with any executive or go into any department—hopefully, with concurrence. Since managers are always apprehensive when reorganization occurs, the organization planners try to keep them informed. This helps create the degree of confidence in organization planning that is required if it is to be effective.

*Aluminum Company of America*

James H. Davis, the department manager at Alcoa, described how an organization director increases his probability of success:

First you do a good job for a fellow, and he comes in for more. After that, his problems are a little more sophisticated. You move up the organization in this way. In the beginning, you deal with works managers, then with division managers, then vice-presidents, and finally the chief executive. Good results and satisfaction in relationships give you new kinds of business.

*The Port of New York Authority*

Harvey Sherman of The Port of New York Authority described how his department evolved from routine administration to major organization analysis:

Our department started with procedures work in the comptroller's department, where we dealt primarily with accounting procedures. Then the department was pulled out of the comptroller's department and assigned to work on all kinds of administrative procedures. Gradually, the relationship between procedures and organization became obvious, and we began to work on organization.

At first the organizational problems were minor; later they became more complex. The shift has been toward more complex, high-level organization problems, more interdepartmental and Port-Authority-wide problems, and fewer intradepartmental ones. We feel that the larger departments should have their own management analysts to handle intradepartmental organization problems. We do train these people, and work with them, and give them advice. But we try to operate primarily at the Port-Authority-wide or interdepartmental level, so far as possible.

A primary accomplishment listed by Mr. Sherman for his department was the performance of organization studies to help facility operations, several of which he described.

We had a problem concerning the organization of our police force. When The Port Authority had only tunnels and bridges to operate, we had a centralized police force. When we expanded to include other types of facilities—airports, marine terminals, and bus and truck terminals, which are now some 23 different facilities—we put what we call net-revenue responsibility at the facility level. Our dilemma was this: If you have one central police force, as we did, not reporting to the facilities managers where they work, how can the managers have net-revenue responsibility? On the other hand, if you break up the force and have 23 separate police forces, how can you maintain uniform standards and the kind of police force that police officers are used to working with?

Our solution was a compromise. The policeman's way of doing his job, which involves training and standards, was left centralized under a control police division. What the policeman does on the job comes under the responsibility of the facility manager. This solution worked pretty well, except for discipline. We originally put discipline in the hands of the facility manager, but the police found this arrangement hard to accept.

Later on, we took responsibility for discipline away from the manager and centralized it. In some respects the police may be regarded as having two bosses, but the plan works well. We make certain, through our training courses, that the men understand the system. They are satisfied; the managers are satisfied.

A second organization analysis concerned the handling of engineering, Mr. Sherman said.

Another type of reorganization concerned our central engineering department, which was used by the line departments. We had many complaints that the engineers were overbuilding—that they were putting too much emphasis on structural integrity and not enough on economics and schedule. We did some case studies and examined 20 engineering projects from beginning to end, studying not only engineering aspects but also the human relations problems.

Analysis of those 20 cases showed us pretty clearly that there were certain kinds of activities that should be decentralized to the line departments, while other kinds should remain in the central engineering department. We didn't impose uniformity. For example, in the supervision of construction we decentralized the function to the aviation and marine terminal department, which operates the airports and piers and docks, but kept the function centralized for the tunnels and bridges and the bus and truck terminals.

We assumed that there was no single ideal pattern. Tunnels and bridges are built to last 300 years or more, and the most important thing is that they **don't** fall down. So we decided to leave this responsibility with the chief engineer, where the best engineering talent was. But a hangar at an airport is built to last only about 20 years because of technological changes, and a crack in the wall is not that important. It is important, however, to get the tenant in on time and to maintain revenues to keep the airport self-supporting. So we decided to decentralize supervision of construction to the line department, which is most involved with the end product and oriented toward meeting deadlines, but less motivated to achieve a building that will last forever or be a monument.

In the case of the terminals department, which operates bus and trucks terminals, we didn't decentralize because they don't have enough work throughout the year. Their work occurs in peaks and valleys, and it would have been uneconomical to staff up for perhaps six months and then not have enough to keep the staff busy for the next six months. These are the kinds of considerations that led us to decisions about when and where to centralize or decentralize.

## Kaiser Aluminum and Chemical Corporation

Carlos Efferson of Kaiser told how his time is divided in organization activities.

Three percent of my time is spent on long-range planning, and 10 percent on designing the ideal organization chart, without reference to people for our company. The remaining 87 percent is spent working with top management to develop a chart that will work, considering the people—once we know what the chart really ought to be. Further, after the decision is made and we agree on this structure with these people, implementation of the structure must be accomplished.

Dr. Efferson described how his department fitted into the changing organization environment at Kaiser.

From 1946 to 1957 we were organized functionally, which limited future growth through diversification. I helped establish the profit-center concept and helped refine the decentralization of the refractories division. Then, in 1957, we set up profit centers for the aluminum division and, later, for the chemicals, real estate, and nickel divisions. At present I am helping the trend toward increasing decentralization within divisions. For example, aluminum will have seven subdivisions, and chemicals three.

We are constantly refining the organization by clarifying line and staff responsibilities at corporate and division levels, placing all reasonable responsibilities within the divisions and keeping only the work done best at corporate level there. We are doing our part to encourage Kaiser's growth with organization to support new products, which involves markets for each division and new businesses at the corporate level. We help encourage flexibility to accommodate growth results by having divisions run by mature men who are responsible for their actions and profits and are adaptable to change. We also try to implement decentralization within the framework of formal planning and control systems.

## UniRoyal, Incorporated

William Wrightnour, vice-president, personnel, at UniRoyal, is very flexible in his approach to organization. He cited many examples of the organization analyses his department performs for the corporation. Typical of the problems he has encountered and of his solutions to them is the following example:

We had the problem that divisions said they must have their own engineering departments "because the central engineering department makes gold-plated buildings that are twice as good as they need to be, and cost twice as much." This problem had been with us for a long time, and finally we faced it.

Because there had been two separate engineering organizations (central and divisional), I suggested that we consider making them one. We took the central engineering department, put the best engineer in the company at the head of it, and made him a vice-president. Then we let him staff up with a coordinator of engineering for each division who was selected by the division, not by him. But the coordinator was on his payroll—with a dotted line to the division's general manager on the organization chart—and the people on the division's engineering staff were on the general manager's payroll, reporting to the coordinator. Many people said we were crazy, that these strategies don't work. The typical question was: "How can you have my engineering people report to a man who doesn't report to me? I'm the general manager." We said, "You select him, that's all." And it's worked.

## A Large Technical Company

The organization department director of a technical company described how his department helped design the organization system so that it meshed with the management style of the company's top executives.

We took top management (the president and all those reporting to him) away from the office for three days, and during that time we attempted to identify the behavioral characteristics of each man. This was done on several occasions with the assistance of professionals who held individual counseling sessions with these executives.

Without initially identifying any individual, we described the behavioral characteristics (in language that everyone could understand) of the top management. This meant stating whether they were dominant or aggressive individuals, and whether the values for that group were high-political- or high-power-oriented. Through this kind of interchange, one of the first things that everybody began to realize is that here we had a group of aggressive, dominant executives who were trying to accomplish a reasonably unified goal. This was one of our problems: Each individual was moving in an independent direction.

After having discussions with each man and interrelating them, we finally got to the point where the group wanted to know everyone's behavioral characteristics. We then identified each man and put his name up for everyone to see. So we started to get the kind of discussion we were hoping for, and without the involvement of a T-group session. I believe it helped a great deal.

The most important thing that I believe we accomplished was an appreciation of the fact that no two individuals are alike. We are supposed to know that we are motivated by different things, have different values, and behave in a different way in certain situations; but sometimes we forget. This had begun to be reflected in our attitudes and relationships with subordinates. Upon going through the entire organization, we found that other men had the same management syndrome. We identified the responsibilities of these people and pointed out the kind of behavior their jobs called for. For example, we found men who were essentially concept-oriented or scientifically oriented and who really weren't interested in people at all; yet their jobs called for them to be continuously engaged in activities that required getting things done through people rather than through personal production. So we asked whether these men should be in these jobs.

We've involved ourselves in value studies of individuals, trying to identify the motivational aspects of why men want to move into particular areas of management. Most of our scientists, for example, want to move into management because they think it carries certain prestige and financial remuneration. But once they become managers, most of them try to delegate their management responsibility, and this causes difficulties. Our analyses of organization and people help solve these types of problems.

## A Large Insurance Company

In this company, organization planning is part of the corporate-planning function. The executive in charge of the group described the early stages of their organization activities:

Our initial assignment was to identify the company's organizational problems and find an organizational plan. We developed devices to give us a quick fix on where the company was and where it was headed.

We designed a 30-page questionnaire dealing with all aspects of the company's operating philosophy. We also developed scales on our products and businesses, beginning with individual life insurance and fixed-dollar annuities, and broadening our scope by adding group insurance, variable annuities, and equity funds; then moving on to auto and homeowner's insurance, workmen's compensation, and financial services. Top executives put a little arrow on the scale to show where they throught the company was at this time and where they thought it would be in ten years.

Several hundred members of top management to whom the questionnaire was administered were asked to express their opinions about the company's insurance investment risks, present and future markets, marketing methods, and relations with the government, employees, and customers. In addition they were asked about organization matters such as the way the organization worked and the relationships of corporate and regional offices.

One organization-planning executive pointed out that the questionnaire and interview used to collect this information were problem-oriented.

After we had amassed the data, we used other techniques to identify problems. First we decided on some basic categories for sorting problems and went to work on the interviews, going through each paragraph and coding all data. Then we worked on a scheme for discussion—a systematic approach to the various aspects of the company's organization. By going through all the data and reshuffling information, with staff assistance, we were able to systematically look at a problem and reach some conclusions about whether it was really a problem and whether we had any recommendations for solving it. After all this, we finally came to grips with the key question: What changes in the formal organizational structure should be made to help us deal with these problems? Then an organization plan was proposed.

This organization plan was geared to solve the problems that we identified and to better point us in the direction of the company's goals as we saw them. We found that a few of our executives differed considerably in their opinions, but most of them believed that a considerable degree of movement from where we were at the time seemed desirable for the future. This indicated that we must organize for change.

We discovered that we were too departmentalized. Too many decisions involved too many people. Our management information system was in bad shape because source data were being developed and maintained in too many departments, and the departments had developed their own sets of information.

We recommended the development of a united management information system and an overall planning group with a planning staff to help management get into a new way of working at various levels. We had the idea that when information was developed for management purposes, the data would be derived from common sources and common sets of assumptions would be built into our planning operations. But we did not face the fact that some of our underlying assumptions were inconsistent, and this influenced our final recommendations.

## Evaluation of the Organization Function

Some organization departments have difficulty in identifying specific accomplishments. If they define their role as "staff adviser" rather than as "service," they probably work primarily through the line executives. They are catalysts, and the executives are the problem solvers. In this role, organization specialists cannot easily identify specific accomplishments.

Organization departments that have a well-destablished service role in their companies are better able to specify accomplishments, but they too find it difficult to evaluate their usefulness. Very often their success is determined as much by how they work as by what they do. Presidents and organization executives of participating companies were asked about formal evaluation of their organization function, and most of them indicated one of the following situations: (1) no formal evaluation; (2) general oral review; (3) written performance appraisal with a few fixed criteria; (4) written performance appraisal with supporting statistics in some detail.

Seventy percent of the organization executives in large companies said they submit written progress reports; two-thirds of those in medium-size firms and one-third in smaller firms submitted such reports.

The presidents were asked if they had ever evaluated the effectiveness of the organization planning and development function or activities within their companies. Fifty-nine percent of those in large companies, 66 percent in medium-size, and 46 percent in small firms said yes. However, approximately half of them said that their evaluations were not formal; 40 percent reported providing general oral reviews; and the remaining 10 percent had formal, written evaluations.

On what basis is an organization department accountable for its performance? Many organization executives feel that evaluation is based entirely on subjective appraisal of their abilities. Dr. Efferson of Kaiser expressed a similar view:

> Evaluation is based on the general impression you make on the five or six men who are closest to your boss. That impression gets to the boss. *How* he gets that impression is a composite of a great number of things. I'm pretty sure it isn't based primarily on statistics of results after an organization change. I would think it would be more subject to other factors—his knowledge of how his vice-presidents and other top executives feel about your helping them, for example. It's also based on his feelings regarding your work—that you have been objective and thorough or have not.

An executive in a technological firm said on this point:

> I think 90 percent of the evaluation is based on the value that your particular chief executive places on your advice—which is entirely subjective evaluation. I've gone through some long conversations with my boss, trying to identify the objective criteria that I believe are somewhat reasonable in terms of gauging my own performance.
>
> But, in the organization area, I think one of the ways I'm measured is on my effectiveness as an agent who assists in getting things accomplished—in communicating with various managers and division managers, in coordinating all the actions that need to occur, and in establishing a schedule for the various activities.

James H. Davis of Alcoa agreed in general, but offered one additional measure of evaluation: obtaining a favorable reaction from executives for whom services are provided.

I'm not sure how I'm evaluated. I've tried to get some accountability objectives or some standards that would have measurement in them. You can begin to get measures when you get down into the mechanical things, but they're usually the more routine parts of an activity, such as comparing plant administrative expenses before we started a reorganization and after we had completed it. But there's a fatal flaw in that line of reasoning, too. My clients evaluate me by inviting me back.

Mr. Davis observed that if the work of his group contributes to a successful organization, the group should be evaluated as effective.

The organization executive of an insurance company held a similar view:

On the whole, I'm evaluated in terms of accomplishment. If the top executives accept a fair number of our recommendations, I think this is a favorable evaluation. If, in the course of the year, we have made commitments to them to get certain things done, and we get them done, I think this is favorable.

There's another evaluation that I personally try to use with the people who work with me: It is based on whether they come up with plans for things that we're undertaking, whether they set a cost for their plans, and whether they get the job done at that cost and within the limits indicated. I try to measure their ability to do the things to which they commit themselves, within the time and cost they have specified.

Harvey Sherman of The Port of New York Authority made a distinction between evaluation of top organization executives and evaluation of organization analysts. He said:

I am evaluated on how strongly my boss agrees with my logic and on the results of his adopting—or not adopting—my recommendations. The times I've impressed him most are when I've gone to him with a memorandum proposing reorganization and when I've been able to say that (*a*) all the people agree with it and (*b*) here are the reasons. He reads it through and says, "This is compelling; it's obvious; I don't know why I didn't think of it myself; let's do it." Whether he ever tests my logic afterward depends on how important the change was and the reactions he gets from others.

With regard to organization analysts, we have fairly detailed performance standards for our men working on projects. They are spelled out in four pages and were developed in a staff meeting by the organization analysts themselves.

An example of detailed performance standards appears in Exhibit 15.

*Accomplishments and Challenges*  143

EXHIBIT 15. *Standards of performance for managers, organization planning (Standard Oil Company [Ohio]).*

Planning, administration, and control

Satisfactory performance has been attained with respect to the administration of this staff function when:

1. Plans for the organization, staffing, compensation, development, and succession of this staff unit are reviewed with the senior vice-president of administration at least annually.
   Changes or corrective actions which have been agreed upon are accomplished within established target limits.
2. Standards of performance have been developed for all key positions reporting directly to the manager, organization-planning staff.
3. Specific objectives and standards of performance are achieved within the limits of approved budgets.
4. There is evidence of effective control of the manpower and staffing in the organization-planning unit.
5. The manager, organization-planning staff, appraises the performance of the managerial and professional personnel reporting directly to him, and of other key men on his staff, and reviews these appraisals annually with the senior vice-president of administration.
    a. There is available at this review:
       (1) A written record of the appraisal of each man (except when the man being appraised assists in the review presentation itself).
       (2) An organization chart which summarizes the appraisals and shows back-up candidates for each position on the chart (except for men assisting in the preparation of the chart).
           (a) At least one of the back-up candidates is classified as ready now, and at least one is a longer-term future replacement expected to be ready after further development or experience.
           (b) An exception to item (a) is the unusual case of a position requiring such a special skill that it is not economically feasible to have a back-up candidate in the employ of the company. In such a case the successor would be expected to be hired from outside the company.
           (c) Candidates from other departments are included to the extent practicable.
       (3) A written development plan or training program for each man upon the organization chart.
    b. A course of action is presented to and approved by the senior vice-president of administration within one month following the appraisal review for any man whose performance was appraised as critically below standard.
    c. A man rated as critically below standard is not continued in his present

position after a second annual appraisal indicating the same performance rating.

    *d.* A review with the senior vice-president of administration is made of each man whose performance has been appraised for two consecutive years as above standard, to determine whether it is desirable to find a new job opportunity for him or to enlarge his managerial responsibilities. If a man whose performance has been appraised for two consecutive years as above standard appears to have potential for a high-level management job, a course of action which is consistent with and may be an acceleration of the written development is approved by the senior vice-president of administration no later than six months after the second appraisal review.

Operations

Satisfactory performance has been attained with respect to executive appraisals and executive inventories when:

1. Annual schedules for meetings to conduct departmental organization reviews, executive appraisals, and corporate organization presentations are set, adjusted as necessary, and carried out at a time satisfactory to all participating principals.
2. Formal charts and supporting reference materials are accurately prepared, using imaginative techniques; suggestions, explanations, and comments are offered as appropriate; and records are kept which are acceptable and helpful in the organization reviews presented to the president, executive vice-president, and senior vice-president of administration by all officers reporting directly to each of them, and in the appraisals of these officers themselves. Follow-up assignments proposed at these review and appraisal meetings are accomplished on schedule and according to expectations.
3. Each officer has been given assistance satisfactory to him in the preparation for, the conduct of, and the follow-up on an annual organization and manpower presentation to the president, executive vice-president, and senior vice-president of administration.
4. A corporate manpower and organization review presentation covering key management positions is made at least annually to the president, executive vice-president, and senior vice-president of administration, and is so conducted that they feel the value of such meetings justifies their continuance.
5. A report has been made near the end of each year, to the executive advisory council, of the organization and key manpower condition of the company; and this report is valuable enough to the officers to justify its repetition in subsequent years.
6. Procedures are in operation for the most efficient storage and retrieval of biographical, appraisal, skills, and formal assessment information for all manpower at or above Hay range 32 (including factor comparison grade 15); and when policy exists and procedures are in operation, for providing such information to qualified persons, within appropriate security requirements.

*Accomplishments and Challenges* 145

7. Appropriate information and advice are provided to assist in the development, coordination, and review of manpower plans and forecasts designed to implement the long-range plans.

Satisfactory performance has been attained by the manager, organization-planning staff, with regard to executive placement, executive recruitment, and development when:

1. Procedures are established and are in efficient operation for developing comprehensive candidate lists for all positions classified at or above Hay range 37, and for providing satisfactory advice in weighing job requirements against candidate qualifications.
2. Procedures exist, and acceptable service and advice are provided, for weighing long- and short-term considerations as to the best corporate utilization of key manpower, particularly as differences occur in the implementation of the K-1 policy concerning interdepartmental transfers.
3. Procedures exist, and are readily applied to a companywide review of possible work assignments for persons in positions of key responsibility who, for reasons not reflecting on their personal conduct, integrity, or loyalty, can no longer be continued in these responsibilities.
4. Assistance satisfactory to each officer requesting it has been provided in arranging for formal recruiting services from outside the company for processing and screening candidates for key openings. Outside recruiting services have been coordinated with internal screening and interviewing procedures so as to minimize the burden of time on the officer. Records of services and costs are kept that help in future decisions to use such services.
5. Personal applications and inquiries from individuals outside the company with regard to executive-level positions are courteously acknowledged within 48 hours of the time they are received by the organization-planning staff. Those appropriate for circulation within the company are sent to key managers for inspection, and are followed up to assure their prompt return. Final acknowledgment is given to those individuals whose files have been circulated, and arrangements are made for further screening where appropriate.
6. Assistance is continually requested by officers and their key managers in reviewing and analyzing the developmental needs of their key subordinates and in formulating, with the help of the manager of training and development, plans which make the best use of company training facilities and information while offering effective and efficient development opportunities for all who might benefit.

Satisfactory performance has been attained by the manager, organization-planning staff, with regard to the preparation of organization charts and assistance in organization structuring when:

1. The Sohio management organization manual containing structural organization charts and committee memberships is maintained in such fashion that revisions are prepared, approved, and distributed within one month of the

effective date of an important organization or committee change. Policy and procedures for distributing the book and revisions exist, and are followed. A historical file of organizational structure and committee assignments is established and maintained so that ready reference can be made, as needed, to previous conditions.
2. Studies of organization and other related areas are made as requested, and are reported on schedule in a manner satisfactory to the person initiating the request. Reference materials and records required to conduct comprehensive organizational studies are kept on hand, or are known to be readily accessible.
3. Requests for advice and consultation with regard to organization structure are promptly and effectively responded to, and the organization-planning staff is consulted with regard to such problems with increased frequency.

Satisfactory performance has been attained by the manager, organization-planning staff, with regard to assessment and other psychological services when:

1. Procedures of highly professional quality for testing and assessing the skills and potentials of experienced managerial and professional personnel who are in the company, or are candidates for employment in key positions, are available and employed according to the needs and schedules of the management of the company; and when such services are requested with increased frequency.
2. Full review and consultation with appropriate members of management are provided by the psychological staff regarding assessment information developed with respect to experienced managerial and professional personnel in the company or being considered for employment.
3. Full review and consultation by members of the psychological staff is provided to experienced managerial and professional personnel who request interview time to learn and reflect on the outcome of assessment programs or sessions in which they participated.
4. Any key management man who so requests is provided promptly with interview time to discuss any work-oriented personnel problems or questions, with assurance of appropriate confidentiality; and when these services are increasingly requested.
5. Special interviews are provided for managerial and professional personnel at management request, or as the result of general corporate needs, to establish or consider reasons for termination, work-related personal problems, or low morale.
6. Well-qualified technical and professional control is exercised over the development and maintenance of tests and other standardized screening procedures used by employee relations and operating department personnel in hiring, promoting, and placing employees at all levels in the company.
7. Qualified professional assistance and consultation are provided to management as requested, or are offered as needed, in the analysis and solution of problems and in the development and application of procedures in all human-factor

*Accomplishments and Challenges* 147

areas, including assessment, appraisal, training, communication, motivation, attitude, morale, interpersonal relationships, and group dynamics.

Satisfactory performance has been attained by the manager, organization-planning staff, with regard to security of corporate information when he has taken prescribed and necessary steps to safeguard information, plans, processes, and other intellectual property of the company within his area of responsibility, and has taken affirmative action to prevent the inadvertent or deliberate disclosure, destruction, or theft of information, plans, processes, or other intellectual property of the company, where such disclosure or loss would be contrary to the company's interest.

---

### Problems and Challenges

Organization problems were examined from two basic points of view—those of the presidents and those of organization executives. The presidents were asked: "What major problems or difficulties have you experienced in your company's organization planning and development?" The executives of organization departments were asked: "What major difficulties have you encountered in carrying out organization planning and development activities?"

*People and Management Problems*

The presidents, especially those who had no organization departments, listed problems that indicated their major concern. Two presidents mentioned a lack of qualified executives in their companies.

> The company's rapid growth has developed opportunities faster than we have been able to find the people to fill the jobs. (Boise Cascade)

> Reassignment of personnel who have not kept pace with the increasing demands of their assignments. (Royal Crown Cola)

Other presidents, again many who have no organization departments, indicated that their major problems were to achieve maximum effectiveness with the company's present executives.

Getting the right man in the right slot, and grouping people with the same or similar chemistry so as to achieve maximum motivation and efficiency. (Dura)

Each manager has his own strengths and weaknesses. Capitalizing on a manager's strengths while maintaining his morale is a major organizational problem. (Electric corporation)

Some presidents—but, interestingly enough, no organization executives—listed as their main problems the accomplishment of specific improvements in management.

Keeping senior executives free from decision making which should be done at a lower level. (Bankers Life)

The problem of defining scope and degree of autonomy—that is, the conflict of centralized versus decentralized control. (Control Data)

Tendency of the organization to increase in size and complexity. Interrelation of functional departments. Obtaining consistent understanding of the objectives and application of principles as between major departments. (Major steel corporation)

### Growth and Change Problems

Many organization executives stated that their major problems in organization planning and development resulted from the size and complexity of their companies.

There is a lack of formal corporationwide organization policies and philosophy because we are so big. (Large metal-products company)

The company is becoming so complex that the president cannot keep in touch with organization problems any more. (Large manufacturing company)

We are no longer able to carry out effective organization studies because we've grown so fast. (Large consumer-goods company)

Many executives attributed their organization problems to rapid recent growth; for example, three presidents stated:

Dynamic growth and rapidly changing requirements in recent years have resulted in almost continuous need for reevaluation of the effectiveness of changes made. [Standard Oil (Indiana)]

## Accomplishments and Challenges

This is an era of rapid change. Modification of goals and quick reaction to new circumstances are constant. This is a major problem. (Medium-size chemical company)

Sometimes growth is so rapid that orderly organization planning becomes extremely difficult, but even in times of such great stress, it is both possible and necessary. (Eastern Airlines)

Many organization executives agreed. Harvey Sherman of The Port of New York Authority said:

The problem is that technology and society are changing so rapidly that it's very difficult to adjust to these changes. There are certain kinds of businesses, and certain kinds of cases, where you'll want to keep your objectives relatively loose and flexible so they can be rapidly adjusted.

Up to a point, it's good to know what your objectives are and to get agreement on them; but this can be pushed too far if your objectives are defined too closely. Take the railroads, for example: They agreed on an objective, but it just happened to be the wrong one. If they had not agreed on it, maybe they would have responded a little more rapidly to changes in the environment. Tremendous organization problems flow from these rapid changes.

Other organization executives were also in agreement on this point. Many said their main problem was change.

Rapid change is our major problem in deciding upon the best organization to fit company needs and objectives. (Small chemical company)

The very rapid growth of our company has made organization planning most difficult. Organization structures are obsolete before being properly implemented. (Large textile manufacturer)

The growth of our company has been very rapid. The management talent is spread very thin, and there is not enough time to devote to planning. (Small electronics firm)

Generally, the rest of the problems cited by participants referred to relationships and obtaining the cooperation of others in accomplishing organization department objectives. As one might expect, these problems were listed primarily by organization executives and related to problems with top management, line management, peers, and operating personnel.

## Top Management Relationships

A common complaint of most staff services is that they do not receive enough support from top management to do their job effectively. Organization planning and development is no different in this respect. Many department heads stated that their chief problem is insufficient support from executives at the top. The following statements are typical.

Getting top management's support. (Large metals company)

Selling the concept and the need for organization planning to management. (Large bank)

There is indifference on the part of top management unless a crisis is pending. (Small scientific firm)

Top managers who are production- and sales-oriented need to be sold on the necessity of organization-development activities on their part. (Large paper company)

Sometimes department executives feel they are involved only at the formal level—after the fact—and not in the real "ball game." For example, two directors said:

I am primarily involved in planning *after* organization decisions are made. (Large metal-products firm)

I am not consulted before organization plans are made. (Large publishing company)

In addition to suffering from lack of support, department executives may get in the middle of political struggles at the top. Three executives cited these problems:

Upper-level power plays and politics which lead to occasional unenlightened self-interest on the part of certain top-level executives; and incomplete understanding of company problems, which starts at the top level. (Small consumer-goods manufacturer)

Personality conflicts and differences in concepts between top people, plus their lack of recognition of the need for definition of plan, responsibility, and authority before plans are implemented. (Medium-size electronics firm)

Difficulties in handling conflicts between the personal objectives and strategies of corporate executives and managers and the corporate objectives that affect organization. (Large glass company)

*Accomplishments and Challenges* 151

## Line Management and Peer Relationships

Relationship problems and challenges can exist even when an organization department receives top management support. In fact, they are the problems most frequently mentioned by department heads. Sometimes these problems are stated generally:

Our major problem is acceptance by line executives. (Large metal-manufacturing firm)

Managers are uncomfortable with organization planning or are not willing to consider it important. Few will look beyond their current operating problems. (Large petroleum company)

It is difficult to get division and corporate line and staff executives to give enough attention to organization development and planning activities, in contrast to the attention they pay to their day-to-day operating problems. (Medium-size publishing company)

Some service department heads have an indifferent attitude toward a function that they feel is an encroachment on their responsibility. (Large mining firm)

Several department heads felt that, beyond lack of interest or support, line managers even resented their work. The department head of a small metals firm said, "The operating people resent what I do as interference in their work," and the department head of a large publishing company stated, "My main problem is the rejection of our ideas by the line at first." The executive of a large electronics firm commented, "The cooperation of line management is not always forthcoming." By contrast, a company president expressed the overall problem as "getting operating and staff groups to understand and accept objectives and techniques of long-range planning."

Attitude change may be the key, as suggested by the organization executive of a medium-size metal-products company when he said, "A major problem is the need to change older philosophies, attitudes, and habit patterns of all levels of managers toward organizational change and selection of personnel."

An organization executive of a large consumer goods firm said that, in organization work, "stretching management's thinking and concentration on positions is critical."

Harvey Sherman of The Port of New York Authority pointed out that the control aspect of organization work is an important factor:

Theoretically, the way we try to make it work is by letting an operating department director make an organization change without my approval. If he makes the change without asking for my advice, however, and it doesn't work, he takes a lot more brunt of the blame than if he had asked me. This means in practice that few significant organization changes are made without asking me. If we disagree, we generally go to the top man, and he makes the decision.

Mr. Sherman illustrated his role as "the man in the middle" on control.

Here is the kind of problem I face. One of the controls that I have is over the creation of new positions. A department director may come to me with a strong recommendation for a new position. So I assign one of my men to look at the program. The section chief involved tells him that he doesn't need an additional person, and he wouldn't know what to do with him. Now I'm in a terrible middle situation. I don't approve the requested position, but of course I can't quote the section chief. I have to find a workload rationalization or some other similar reason for turning it down.

Another example is the executive who tells me he needs a certain report. We're trying to reduce reports, but he says this one is essential. I talk to his secretary; she says that she files them but her boss never reads them. But I don't want to cause her trouble by quoting her. In this kind of work you have these kinds of problems, but it's all part of the job.

Another problem of the organization executive is keeping confidences. Carlos Efferson of Kaiser remarked about this:

A big difficulty is that a top manager often discusses his organization problems with the organization specialist fully and in complete confidence, and this can involve delicate situations. For example, he gets into matters relating to men who aren't doing their jobs. The top manager may not want to confide such matters; but he feels he must talk to someone, and often it is the organization man. Afterward he crosses his fingers and hopes the organization man will not tell, or show by his actions, what the top manager thinks before he has a chance to do what he has to do about it.

There aren't too many people of this stature in a division who can command this kind of confidence. In a number of companies what often happens is that the division or plant-level organization specialist is really a procedures man. Then the division manager goes to someone else—his priest, or the corporation organization man, or somebody else—to talk over the things that are most important to organization thinking.

*Accomplishments and Challenges* 153

Another organization executive of a large metals firm summarized this problem as follows:

At times, studies of significant organization changes must be conducted on a highly confidential basis. Accordingly, useful information and opinions cannot be secured directly, if at all, and must be handled carefully.

## Middle Management Relationships

The final set of problems experienced primarily by organization executives involved difficulty in implementing organization recommendations or changes. This may be caused by inadequate staff. One organization executive said his main problem was lack of available time and staff. And, in a medium-size metal-assembly company, the executive stated his problem as lack of adequate assistance at operating levels.

A more frequent complaint cited general problems concerning implementation or resistance to change, such as the following:

People problems related to developing and implementing organization changes. The best structure cannot always be implemented—for reasons of personality, lack of skills, or other. (Large petroleum company)

Obtaining a consensus concerning a change. A tendency of departments to have organization-planning activity follow instead of precede other considerations. A tendency to deviate from organization plans to the point where conflicts in assignments and responsibilities appear. (Medium-size metals manufacturer)

Conflicts that arise in attempting to reconcile sound organization with available personnel. (Large manufacturing company)

Donald Taffi of Electro-Optical Systems pointed out that implementation is an especially difficult problem:

We had gone through a major reorganization, a year before, which we spent four months trying to implement. When we actually completed the implementation a year later, we asked this group of people to tell us about their jobs, and we found out that in fact the new organization was still the old organization. We discovered that most of our managers were still going to where they knew they could get the job done, and contacting men whom they should no longer contact because they knew them. The new organization existed only on a chart.

Most respondents categorized this kind of problem as resistance to change. Two presidents mentioned it specifically.

Resistance to change is the greatest difficulty. (Northwestwern Mutual Life Insurance Company)

Resistance to change, particularly the resistance of individual managers to giving up areas for which they have previously had responsibility, is frequently a great problem and one that must be dealt with firmly. (Alan Wood Steel)

Organization executives reported problems of:

Resistance to change and new concepts. (Large chemical company)

Bringing about change and breaking with tradition. (Large textile firm)

Normal resistance to analysis, evaluation, and/or change. (Medium-size paper firm)

Providing people the time to prepare for change and acceptance of change. (Large scientific firm)

Reluctance to make necessary changes because of individual personalities and individual personal situations. (Medium-size metals firm)

Attitudes created by former corporate policy which had established the company as a decentralized operation. (Medium-size consumer-goods manufacturer)

As expected, organization-planning departments listed as their major accomplishments structural analysis and changes leading to more efficient organizations. Organization-development departments listed accomplishments that integrated structural and human changes and improvements.

Major problems seen by the presidents tended to be specific organization problems, such as the need to decentralize, or improvement in managerial talents. Sometimes their focus was on the difficulty of providing adequate organization and climate in a fast-changing world.

In contrast, the organization executives seemed concerned with more immediate problems, such as relationships, lack of support by top management and line executives, and difficulties in implementing changes.

These differences in orientation may help to explain the lack of effectiveness of organization planning and development that is experienced by so many industrial and nonindustrial companies today. As the president of one participating company assessed the situation, "The major problems and difficulties have been to make organization planning and development more than lip service and resolutions in favor of virtue. It must be an effective, action-producing, problem-solving function."

# Appendix A

# Historical Antecedents of the Organization Function

Organization as a separate field of study has interested men throughout history, and most of the great civilizations produced literature on the subject. The Egyptians, Assyrians, Greeks, Romans, Chinese, Arabs, and Prussians were interested in the organization of society and government. For hundreds of years, European historians have studied the organization of the church and the military. After the Industrial Revolution, the English began to study their textile firms and other business enterprises. In America, early concepts were strongly influenced by the organization of the railroad companies, which were the largest enterprises at that time.

During the past 50 years, managers regarded organization problems as part of their job, and they handled them personally. Sometimes they sought help from their colleagues. Occasionally, this relationship was formalized and an ad hoc committee was established to solve a specific organization problem. After the problem had been solved, the committee was dissolved. In the 1920s this method was used in reorganization at Du Pont, General Motors Corporation, Sears, Roebuck & Company, and Standard Oil Company (New Jersey), as Alfred D. Chandler Jr. has described it in *Strategy and Structure*. (Books and articles cited in Appendix A are listed in Appendix B under the heading, "Selected Reading.")

Companies with a need for continual organizational activities delegated this responsibility to one person on either a part-time or full-time basis. In some cases, these staff members had administrative duties, and in others they served as corporate consultants on organization problems. Outside management consultants also provided companies with assistance. Prior to World War II, a few corporations had actually established organization departments. One of the first to do so was Standard Oil Company of California (1931).

A number of businessmen and scholars have advocated that large companies establish organization departments. In 1941 Paul Holden, Lounsberry Fish, and H. L. Smith stated this opinion in *Top Management Organization Planning and Control,* one of the more important early books on organization.

Good [organization] practice provides for comprehensive, long-range organization planning, rationalization of the structure as a whole, proper design and clarification of each part, competent review of proposed changes, and periodic checks of actual organization practice.

This is the logical province of a competent staff department specializing in organization problems, working through the medium of a well-designed organizational manual.

These authors conducted studies in 30 West Coast firms, four of which had organization departments. They concluded that an organization department should perform the following activities:

... determine needs, formulate plans, and secure acceptance, cooperation, and support to the ends of: (1) the best possible organization to meet the goals; (2) appropriate functions, objectives, and relationships and limits of authority clarified and defined for levels, departments, and jobs; (3) size of manpower kept to a minimum to handle the work.

Also in the 1940s Alvin Brown, a leading businessman, frequently cited the need for a formalized organization function. He hoped that business schools would begin to teach organization as a function and that companies would create organization departments to utilize this knowledge.

Charles R. Hook, Jr., vice-president of industrial relations of the Chesapeake & Ohio Railroad, maintained that personnel problems are closely related to broader problems. Accordingly, he decentralized his function by assigning personnel men to the company's divisions as department representatives. One of their main functions was organization. However, he admitted that in organization planning he had "made the mistake of allowing glittering mechanistic principles to outweigh realities."

In contrast to Messrs. Holden, Fish, and Smith (who emphasized structure as the focus of organization work) Mr. Hook believed that the focus of personnel work should be on people. He summarized his viewpoint as follows in an article, "Organization Planning: Its Challenges and Limitations":

Above all, an organization is people—not a collection of functions. Too much of the thinking devoted to organization planning has been done as though we were embarking upon the structuring and staffing of a brand-new but as yet nonexistent organization. If this were the case, our problems would be simple indeed! Under such a situation, it is not only possible but almost imperative that our planning should be carried out without regard to any particular human being. Aren't most of us concerned with the improvement of an *already existing* organization, a *living,* breathing organization?

Mr. Hook was convinced that organization work failed if it did not receive line support, if the organization planner did not involve the line, or if too much reliance were put on "the plan"—that is, on one specific method of structuring an organization.

In 1952 Ernest Dale's *Planning and Developing the Company Organization Structure* combined classical organization theory with a detailed analysis of current organization practices. Dr. Dale conducted meetings with a group of organization planners to gather information and evaluate his research. From these meetings evolved an association for organization analysts: the Organization Development Council in New York. Later, the Council on Organization Planning of the National Industrial Conference Board (now known as the Conference Board) in New York and the West Coast Organization Planning Round Table in San Francisco were founded. Dr. Dale's book, written for both organization specialists and line managers, influenced many executives and stimulated the establishment of organization departments in a number of companies. The success of this book prompted Dr. Dale to revise it, and the American Management Association to publish the revised edition, in 1967.

The development of organization departments has been influenced by AMA and the Conference Board, which published a number of studies on organization during the 1950s. Louis Allen ("Organization Planning") wrote rather extensively on the subject, as did Carlos Efferson, an industrial psychologist now vice-president of organization planning at Kaiser. When Dr. Efferson created an organization-planning department for Kaiser, he visited 15 companies known to have such departments. He found few patterns because the departments were new and had developed out of several others. He later commented in an article, "Some Basic Considerations in Organization Planning":

As a national pattern, organization planning seems literally to be whatever you call it; and an organization-planning man is whomever the firm chooses for the job, and his previous experience is typically unrelated to organization planning. Finally, organization planning seems to consist of whatever these people decide to do.

Dr. Efferson concluded that a successful organization department must fit the norms of the company it serves. At Kaiser, it was project-oriented and not involved in routine administration. It provided staff services to improve the organizational ability of line managers and acted as a catalytic agent by helping them find solutions to organization problems for presentation to their supervisors for approval.

During the 1960s, interest in organization departments continued, but the emphasis shifted to evaluation of the function's usefulness. In their book, *Administrative Organization,* John Pfiffner and Frank Sherwood advocated the use of organization departments. Most of their information about such departments came from Kaiser and from Standard Oil Company of California. Professors Pfiffner and Sherwood described organization planning as a top-level coordinating activity with a broad planning orientation. They pointed out that this function was far more useful to an organization than "management analysis," the activity being performed by many government departments, since the latter quickly bogged down in details and low-level activities.

Successful experiences of other companies' organization departments were presented in *Organization Theory in Industrial Practice,* edited by Mason Haire, a professor at M.I.T. In this book, organization executives from Bell Telephone Company of Pennsylvania, Union Carbide, General Electric Company, and others described the activities of their departments and discussed successful organization changes initiated, implemented, or advised by their departments. Professor Haire was somewhat critical of their efforts, commenting that organization-department heads presumably try to consider the best organization for their firm but that he wondered how they determine which is best. To make a choice among alternatives, one must first know the objectives the structure is designed to attain and how it will attain them. Professor Haire sees the job of organization departments as difficult and perhaps impossible.

AMA and the Conference Board have continued to study organization. However, the first extensive survey of departments was conducted by Joseph Bailey in 1964 and reported in "Organization: Whose Responsibility?" Of the companies that participated in the survey, 61 had separate organization departments and 98 had organization activities assigned to another department. However, these classifications overlapped: Among the separate organization departments were listed personnel administration and industrial relations. Only 39 of the companies had departments whose titles indicated that they were concerned exclusively with organization, and 20 had titles that joined organization with another activity, usually personnel. The 98 companies with joint departments were also usually a combination of organization and some personnel function. A few combined organization and corporate planning or development, and nine firms combined organization and financial or engineering activities.

Harold Leavitt, an organization psychologist, provided two contrasting viewpoints in two editions of his book, *Managerial Psychology.* In the 1958 edition he described the potentially important role of organization departments as follows:

Organizations can build internal eyes on themselves . . . in several ways. A department of organization (a relatively rare phenomenon today) can serve such a purpose. It can search continually for the problems the mother structure is creating—for gaps in authority, or for overlapping authority. It can watch for red flags from departments that are getting excessively squeezed by the organization structure. It can look for places where committees can operate better than individuals, and individuals better than committees. It can feed back to the brains of the organization some information about the effects of the organization's own behavior. Unfortunately, many departments of organization don't do these jobs. They draw charts instead.

In the 1964 edition of his book, Dr. Leavitt admitted that, in theory, organization analysis can contribute more to a company than he had assumed previously; yet he did not discuss the contribution of departments. He emphasized the importance of structure as follows:

The great early emphasis of structural people on authority led us for a while toward rejecting the whole structural approach. We tended, as we so often do, to want to throw out the baby with the bath water. Recently, we have begun to come back to structural questions from very different angles. We have come back to structure, largely because we have been forced to—because it became so patently obvious that structure is an organization dimension (1) that we can manipulate; (2) that has direct effects on problem solving.

If we decentralize, things happen. Maybe not all the things we wanted to have happen, but things happen. If we change communication lines by removing telephones, or separating people, or making some people inaccessible to others, things happen.

All of those kinds of changes are fairly easy for managers to carry out. So the structural dimensions became doubly important—important because they constrain and thereby influence behavior—important because they are readily manipulatable.

More recently, the author of this report studied the current activities and accomplishments of organization departments in seven companies and concluded that the most effective departments were those that combined organization activities with certain aspects of personnel, especially management development, manpower planning, and motivation and compensation.

The most popular ideas about organization analysis and change have emanated from organization-development specialists who are primarily interested in improving organization through changing and redirecting its members. The result has been increased use of T-group training, grid training, and structured organization-development programs by organization departments and/or with the use of outside consultants or programs.

# Appendix B

# Selected Reading

THE items in the following list were chosen as representing a limited but good-quality selection of publications about organization planning and development.

*1. Importance and Need*

Daniel, D. Ronald, "Reorganizing for Results." *Harvard Business Review,* November–December 1966, pp. 96–104.

Hershey, Robert L., "Organizational Planning." *MSU Business Topics,* Winter 1962, pp. 29–40.

Janger, Allen R., *Personnel Administration: Changing Scope and Organization.* New York: National Industrial Conference Board, Studies in Personnel Policy 203, 1967.

McFarland, Dalton, *Company Officers Assess the Personnel Function.* AMA, Research Study 79, 1967.

Miles, Raymond E., "The Affluent Organization." *Harvard Business Review,* May–June 1966, p. 106.

*2. Early Studies*

Allen, Louis, "Organization Planning." *Management Record,* October 1954, pp. 1–7.

Blau, Peter, *Bureaucracy in Modern Society.* New York: Random House, 1956.

———, and Scott, W. Richard, *Formal Organizations.* San Francisco: Chandler Publishing Company, 1962.

Brown, Alvin, "Organization as a Separate Branch of Management." *Annual Proceedings,* Academy of Management, December 30, 1949.

Dale, Ernest, *Planning and Developing the Company Organization Structure.* AMA, 1952. Revised edition, 1967.

Efferson, Carlos, "Organization Planning for Management Growth." *Management Record,* April 1958, p. 134.

———, "Some Basic Considerations in Organization Planning." *Academy of Management Journal,* April 1959, p. 31.

Holden, Paul E., Fish, Lounsbury S., and Smith, Hubert L., *Top Management Organization and Control.* New York: McGraw-Hill, 1951, pp. 12–13.

Hook, Charles R., Jr., "Organization Planning: Its Challenges and Limitations." AMA, Personnel Series 141, 1951, pp. 15–22.

Rice, A. K., *Productivity and Social Organization.* London: Tavistock Institute, 1958.

Trickett, Joseph, "Organization Planning." *Advanced Management Journal,* March 1948.

## 3. Later Studies

Bailey, Joseph, "Organization Planning: Whose Responsibility?" *Academy of Management Journal,* June 1964, pp. 96–108.

Glover, John, and Lawrence, Paul, *A Case Study of High-Level Administration in a Large Organization.* Cambridge, Mass.: Harvard University Press, 1964.

Glueck, William F., "Applied Organization Analysis." *Academy of Management Journal,* September 3, 1967, pp. 223–234.

———, *Organization Development Departments in Selected American Firms: An Exploratory Behavioral Analysis.* Ann Arbor, Mich.: University Microfilms, 1966.

———, "Where Organization Planning Stands Today." *Personnel,* July–August 1967, pp. 19–26.

Haire, Mason, ed., *Organization Theory in Industrial Practice.* New York: John Wiley & Sons, 1962.

Katz, Daniel, and Kahn, Robert L., *The Social Psychology of Organizations.* New York: John Wiley & Sons, 1966.

Litterer, Joseph, *The Analysis of Organizations.* New York: John Wiley & Sons, 1965.

Perna, Joseph A., "Organization Structure and Practices of Large U.S. Corporations." M.B.A. thesis. Detroit: Wayne State University, 1966.

Pfiffner, John, and Sherwood, Frank, *Administrative Organization.* New York: Prentice-Hall, 1960.

———, "Dimensions of Organization Structure." *Administrative Science Quarterly,* June 1968, pp. 65–105.

Scott, William G., *Organization Theory.* Homewood, Ill.: Richard D. Irwin, 1967.

Stieglitz, Harold, *Organization Planning: Basic Concepts and Emerging Trends.* New York: National Industrial Conference Board, 1962.

Tannenbaum, Robert, et al., *Leadership and Organization.* New York: McGraw-Hill, 1961.

## 4. Current Studies with Impact for the Future

Argyris, Chris, *Integrating the Individual and the Organization.* New York: John Wiley & Sons, 1964.

———, "T-Groups for Organizational Effectiveness," *Harvard Business Review,* March–April 1964.

Beckhard, Richard, *Organization Development: Strategies and Models.* Reading, Mass.: Addison-Wesley, 1969.

Bennis, Warren G. (edited by E. Schein, et al.) *Organization Development: Its Nature, Origins, and Prospects.* Reading, Mass.: Addison-Wesley, 1969.

Blake, Robert, et al., "Breakthrough in Organization Development." *Harvard Business Review,* November–December 1965, p. 133.

Blake, Robert, and Mouton, Jane, *Organizational Development Through the Managerial Grid.* Reading, Mass.: Addison-Wesley, 1969.

———, *The Managerial Grid.* Houston, Texas: Gulf Publishing Company, 1964.

Burns, Tom, and Stalker, G. M., *The Management of Innovation.* New York: Barnes & Noble, 1961.

Cartwright, Dorwin, "Influence, Leadership, Control." In *Handbook on Organizations,* edited by James G. March. New York: Rand McNally, 1965, pp. 1–47.

Chandler, Alfred D., Jr., *Strategy and Structure.* New York: Doubleday, 1966.

Chapple, Eliot D., and Sayles, Leonard R., *The Measure of Management.* New York: Macmillan, 1961.

Fiedler, Fred E., *A Theory of Leadership Effectiveness.* New York: McGraw-Hill, 1967.

———, *Toward a Contingency Theory of Leadership.* New York: McGraw-Hill, 1967.

Gardner, John, "How to Prevent Organization Dry Rot." *Harper's Magazine,* October 1965.

Greiner, Larry E., "Patterns of Organization Change." *Harvard Business Review,* May–June 1967, pp. 119–130.

Hickson, D. J., et al., "Operations Technology and Organization Structure: An Empirical Reappraisal." *Administrative Science Quarterly,* Vol. 14, No. 2, 1969.

Hill, Walter A., and Egan, Douglas, *Readings in Organization Theory.* Boston: Allyn and Bacon, 1966.

Lawrence, Paul, and Lorsch, Jay, *Organization and Environment.* Cambridge, Mass.: Harvard University Press, 1968.

———, *Organization Intervention.* Reading, Mass.: Addison-Wesley, 1969.

Leavitt, Harold, "Applied Organization Change in Industry." In *Handbook on Organizations,* op. cit., pp. 1144–1170.

———, *Managerial Psychology.* Chicago: University of Chicago Press, 1958, pp. 281–282. Second edition, 1964, p. 387.

Likert, Rensis, *The Human Organization.* New York: McGraw-Hill, 1968.

Pugh, Derek, et al., "A Conceptual Scheme of Organization Analyses." *Administrative Science Quarterly,* March 1963, pp. 289–315.

Rubenowitz, Sigvard, "Personnel Management Organization in Some European Societies." *Management International Review,* 1968/4–5, pp. 74–92.

Schein, Edgar H., *Process Consultation in Organizational Development.* Reading, Mass.: Addison-Wesley, 1969.

Shepard, Herbert A., "Changing Interpersonal and Intergroup Relationships in Organizations." In *Handbook on Organizations,* op. cit., pp. 1115–1143.

Sherman, Harvey, *It All Depends.* University of Alabama Press, 1966.

Sofer, Cyril, *The Organization from Within.* Tavistock Publications, Barnes & Noble, 1961.

Walton, Richard, *Interpersonal Peacemaking: Confrontations and Third-Party Consultation in Organizational Development.* Reading, Mass.: Addison-Wesley, 1969.

Woodward, Joan, *Industrial Organization: Theory and Practice.* McGraw-Hill, 1968.

Zaleznik, Abraham, "Interpersonal Relations in Organizations." In *Handbook on Organizations,* op. cit., pp. 574–613.